BOYS TOWN

A PHOTOGRAPHIC HISTORY

THE
DONNING COMPANY
PUBLISHERS

BOYS TOWN
A PHOTOGRAPHIC HISTORY

"HE AIN'T HEAVY, FATHER... HE'S M'BROTHER"

BOYS TOWN

DEDICATED TO HELPING ALL YOUTH
REALIZE THEIR FULL POTENTIAL
FOR GOD, SELF, AND SOCIETY

BARBARA A. LONNBORG, EDITOR

        The Boys Town Press
        Father Flanagan's Boys' Home
        Boys Town, Nebraska 68010

At the Donning Company/Publishers:
Elizabeth B. Bobbitt, Coordinator and Editor
Barbara A. Bolton, Project Director
Lori J. Wiley, Art Director, Designer

Library of Congress Cataloging-in-Publication Data

Boys Town: a photographic history/Barbara A. Lonnborg, editor.
        p.   cm.
    Includes index.
    ISBN 0-938510-31-2 (hardcover: alk. paper)
    1. Father Flanagan's Boys Home—History—Pictorial works. 2. Boys—Institutional care—Nebraska—Boys
Town—History—20th century—Pictorial works. 3. Orphanages—Nebraska—Boys Town—History—20th
century—Pictorial works. 4. Flanagan, Edward Joseph, 1886–1948—Pictorial works. I. Lonnborg, Barbara.
II. Father Flanagan's Boys Home.
HV876.B65   1992
362.7'4'09782254—dc20   92-18878
                                                                                CIP

4

Printed in the United States of America

CONTENTS

ACKNOWLEDGMENTS

Many people made great contributions to the creation of this book. They are: Joan Flinspach, Tom Lynch, and Ralph Wright whose research provided the backbone of this work; Cheryl Sacco and Hugh Reilly who wrote sections of the manuscript; Tom Gregory, Dave Coughlin, Dan Daly, Bernie Devlin, and Randy Blauvelt who read many drafts of the manuscript and offered valuable suggestions; Ed Novotny and Frank Szynskie who contributed memories and photographs as alumni and longtime employees of Boys Town; John Melingagio who provided and helped locate many contemporary photographs; Steve Szmrecsanyi who conducted oral history interviews with alumni and former employees; Jo Behrens who compiled a timeline of the Home's early years; Mary Sundvold who spent many hours on the computer revising the manuscript; forty Hall of History volunteers, chief among them Erna Andersen, LaVern Lenzen, William and Darlene Teachman, and Virginia Thimes, who donated months of effort sorting, identifying, and filing the more than two hundred fifty thousand prints and negatives in the Boys Town photographic archives; and the many Boys Town youth whose work in the Hall of History greatly enhances its services to staff, alumni, and visitors.

Father Edward J. Flanagan, founder and director of Boys Town from 1917 to 1948.

BOYS TOWN

An Irish Immigrant

"Leabeg House, ancestral home of the Flanagans in Ireland, was not unlike other rural homes of the day in Southern County Roscommon. . . .There were eleven of us children, four boys and seven girls. Alexander Graham Bell's telephone was still a curiosity. The automobile was unknown, as was the airplane, the radio, the 'talkies,' and a great many other modern conveniences we look now upon as necessities," Father Flanagan once said of his youth in Ireland.

Born on July 13, 1886, Edward Joseph Flanagan was plagued by poor health from his first days. Unable to play or work as hard as his siblings, he became a reader and an observer. John and Nora Flanagan—people of modest means and deep faith—hoped their son would one day become a Catholic priest, so they strived to educate him in the best schools. Young Flanagan, too, wanted desperately to enter the priesthood.

Late in the summer of 1904, Edward Flanagan boarded the S.S. *Celtic* destined for America, where he hoped to enter the seminary and begin his life as a priest. Within two years he had earned his undergraduate degree from Mount St. Mary's College in Emmitsburg, Maryland. Once in New York at St. Joseph's Seminary, however, Flanagan found his goal would not be obtained easily—a lesson he would learn over and over again in his work. A St. Joseph's staff member judged him in 1907 to be a "nice little gentleman, but delicate in health. . . just fair in talents." A bout with double pneumonia kept Flanagan out of classes for months, and the weakened state of his lungs eventually convinced the seminary he could not withstand the rigors of another term.

Brothers Edward and P.A. Flanagan (first row, third and fourth from left) sailed to America aboard the S.S. *Celtic*, White Star Line, in 1904.

Flanagan's parents had emigrated in 1906 and were also living in New York. They and Edward decided to move to Omaha, Nebraska, where an older son, Patrick, was a parish priest. Following Patrick's introduction, the local bishop saw more promise in Edward the aspiring priest, and the diocese gave Flanagan an opportunity to study at Gregorian University in Rome in the fall of 1907. A cold, wet, treacherous winter in Rome, however, brought on a recurrence of respiratory illness and by February 1908, Flanagan

Circa 1908, John and Nora Flanagan pose with eight of their eleven children, including (front row, from left) Edward, Michael, P.A., (back row, from left) Delia, Theresa, James, Nellie, and Susan. For many years Nellie was Father Flanagan's housekeeper at Boys Town.

was forced to return to Omaha to recuperate.

For more than a year, the dispirited young man struggled to regain his health, working in the accounting department of the Cudahy Meat Packing Company in Omaha. In 1909 the Bishop of Omaha sent young Edward to the dry mountain air of Innsbruck, Austria, where he enrolled in the famous university's department of theology and resumed his quest for the priesthood.

Three years later, on the feast of St. Anne, July 26, 1912, Edward J. Flanagan was ordained a priest in Innsbruck. Scarcely a month later, he returned to the United States where John and Nora Flanagan watched with joy as their son celebrated his first Solemn High Mass of Thanksgiving at Holy Angels Church in Omaha. For them, the dream was complete. For Father Flanagan, it was just beginning.

The Early Work

After a brief assignment in O'Neill, Nebraska, Father Flanagan returned to Omaha to serve at St. Patrick's Church. In 1915 the city seemed to be inundated with homeless, jobless, and hungry men. A poor farm economy had sent thousands of men to the city in search of work. Many got off the train in Omaha and wandered the city streets looking for work and food. They found no work, no shelter, little food, and no hope. In desperation, hundreds of these men went to the city's churches with their plight. Many parishes would provide a meal, but none had the resources to help so many men in need.

Watching the escalating problem and numbers of homeless and unemployed men, Father Flanagan enlisted the aid of the St. Vincent dePaul Society, which

The old Burlington Hotel at Eleventh and Mason streets in Omaha served as Father Flanagan's first Workingmen's Hotel.

agreed to lease a vacant hotel as a temporary residence where he could provide meals, lodging, and work for men in need. The forty cots in Father Flanagan's Workingmen's Hotel were filled almost immediately after opening day in January 1916, and the demand grew daily. As he would do many times later, Father Flanagan appealed to the public to help him help others. The result this time was sixty more cots, clothing, and shoes for his residents. Only six weeks after the hotel opened, twenty of the men had landed permanent jobs while many others were doing temporary work.

Archbishop Jeremiah Harty transferred Father Flanagan to a different parish so he would be able to devote even more time to the hotel, which had since moved to a more spacious location. The new hotel boasted three hundred beds, reading, and other activities for the residents, plus an "employment agency" that by the end of 1917 had secured over fifteen hundred jobs for the residents. Although the hotel kept thousands of transient men off the streets of Omaha, Father Flanagan often felt discouraged by how difficult it was for these men to make lasting changes in their lives. He wrote:

> I knew. . . that my life's work lay in the rehabilitation of these men. And yet, my methods were so basically wrong. . . . In talking with the men, I learned that they had been orphaned in childhood. . . .Or, they were members of large families where income was not sufficient to care for them.

Father Flanagan, at left, with St. Patrick's parishioners in O'Neill, Nebraska, his first parish assignment in 1912.

. . . Or, again, they [came] from families broken by divorce. Invariably they were homeless and abandoned. . . . They veered here, were shoved there throughout their formative years and, reaching a man's estate, were only shells of men. . . . I knew that my work was not with these shells of men, but with the embryo men—the homeless waifs who [had] nowhere to turn, no one to guide them.

So Father Flanagan set out to find a way to care for boys rather than men.

A Boys' Home

There were plenty of delinquent and homeless boys roaming Omaha's streets in 1917. Some were orphaned, some were runaways, and the only fault of others was being born into a poor family that could not care for or feed them. The courts were desperate to find places to send young boys who had been charged with stealing bread or money from the corner store.

Archbishop Harty relieved Father Flanagan of his parish duties on December 12, 1917, so he could concentrate fully on his new mission of operating a home for boys such as these. Father Flanagan turned to a trusted friend to borrow the ninety dollars needed to pay the first month's rent for a large house in downtown Omaha. Although he kept his promise not to reveal his friend's identity, it is all but certain the gift came from Henry Monsky, a prominent Jewish attorney active in the Boy Scouts and Juvenile Court. Monsky shared his friend's concern for youngsters who were being shuffled through the court system, only to come out on the other end bitter and with no more direction than they had before. Henry Monsky did not share the same religion as Father Flanagan, but he did share many of the same beliefs—most importantly that faith, education, and kindness could change a young boy's life.

Flanagan opened his Home in a rented building at 106 North Twenty-fifth Street.

The First Christmas

Less than two weeks before Christmas 1917, Father Flanagan and his first residents walked through the doors of a rickety home on Twenty-fifth and Dodge streets. World War I had created scarcities in most homes across the country.

Father Flanagan's was no different. The ninety dollars had only paid for one month's rent and, with boys arriving daily—from the courts, off the streets, and from referrals by sympathetic citizens—Father Flanagan was hard-pressed to provide food and clothing. Archbishop Harty had arranged for two nuns and a novice from the School Sisters of Notre Dame to help cook, clean, sew, and care for the boys. On the morning of Christmas Eve, however, Father Flanagan had nothing for the nuns to cook for his family of boys numbering nearly twenty-five. But, as he would experience time and again, someone stepped in to help just when things seemed hopeless. An Omaha merchant delivered a barrel of sauerkraut that Christmas Eve.

"It was a rather humble festival," Father Flanagan said, "but we were happy and determined to make a success of our small institution."

The German-American Home

Donations from friends and support from the public made the following months easier. Food was more plentiful; all the boys had clean clothes and shoes on their feet, and a horse and wagon had been rented to transport the boys to school and church. By the spring of 1918, Father Flanagan found himself in charge of about one hundred boys. Not only was the Home growing in popula-

Five of the boys in residence at Father Flanagan's Boys' Home on January 19, 1918.

tion, but also in popularity. Support for Father Flanagan's undertaking was overwhelmingly evident on April 11, 1918, when four thousand people attended the Home's first annual benefit dinner, helping to raise more than fifty-three hundred dollars.

The boys' quarters were becoming cramped and the fund-raising dinner had allowed Father Flanagan a larger

Two years after opening his Home Father Flanagan had almost a hundred boys in residence at the former German-American Home, 4206 South Thirteenth Street.

budget, so a search was begun for a new home. He was able to rent the city's German-American Home inexpensively. Father Flanagan found it to be a more than suitable home for his boys of every race and religion. Their new home was spacious, complete with playground, bowling alley, and pool tables in the basement. These were important considerations in Father Flanagan's search for a new home. While he expected all the boys to complete their schoolwork and chores, there was always time for play—Father Flanagan made sure of it. "Some of the finest people in the world go through life under a handicap because they never learned how to play when they were children," he said.

Charity balls came only once a year and hungry boys arrived daily at the Home, so vegetables were planted immediately and Father Flanagan began asking monthly for livestock through his *Father Flanagan's Boys' Home Journal*, a monthly publication begun in 1918 to inform the public about the Home's activities and to solicit support. One such request read: ". . . we just hate to be buying canned milk and we can't afford fresh milk, so if we had a cow we could possibly have all the milk that she would supply us." More than a year passed before his requests for livestock were answered by a local farmer who donated a pig. It was eaten scarcely a month later, and Father Flanagan continued to ask monthly for "a pig or two" or a milk cow.

In the early years, limited resources prevented Father Flanagan from hiring more than a few staff members at very low wages. Many of his own family members, including his mother, his sister Nellie, and Patrick and Lenora Norton, a nephew and niece, supplied much of the desperately needed labor along with nuns from several different orders.

All Creeds and Colors

From the beginning, Father Flanagan accepted boys of all creeds and color. A black boy got as hungry as a white boy and an alley didn't make a better bed for a Jewish boy than a Catholic one. An immigrant himself, Father Flanagan believed passionately that the American ideals of freedom, equality, and justice were words to be practiced, not just preached. "I see no disaster threatening us because of any particular race, creed, or color," Father Flanagan said. But he did see "danger for all in an ideology which discriminates against anyone politically or economically" because he was born into a different race or worshiped at a different altar.

Father Flanagan's boys were no strangers to intolerance. They were teased or shunned at the public schools because they dressed shabbily and had poor academic skills. Many had been abandoned by their parents and had attended school only sporadically. Now, however, they faced a more dangerous opposition in the early 1920s. Father Flanagan had organized an interracial group of boys to travel the Midwest to spread the message of the Home and raise funds through entertainment. "The World's Greatest Juvenile Entertainers" performed two-hour shows, pleasing their audiences with songs, skits, jokes, and speeches. In 1922 the boys traveled to their engagements in bright red, second-hand circus wagons. In later years they journeyed by train in their own special Pullman car. Father Flanagan's nephew, Patrick Norton, chaperoned the boys while an agent booked as many shows as the boys could travel to on weekends and during the summer. Communities were anxious to see Father Flanagan's boy performers. But not every community was filled with supportive admirers of this integrated family.

"I recall one incident," Norton remembered, "where a minister who had joined the Ku Klux Klan advised us that if we put on our show in that community, he would tar and feather all of us." Through the years, hotels in Miami, Washington, D.C., Baltimore, and many other cities across the coun-

Some early residents of the Home.

try would invite the well-known boy musicians and athletes from Father Flanagan's home to visit, only to rescind the invitation when they discovered that the group was racially mixed.

School and a Trade

Once home, the boys continued working side by side in the garden, sharing sleeping quarters and eating together, oblivious to their differences. Some of the boys were having trouble in the public schools. Occasionally the boys were not accepted because of their backgrounds and delinquent pasts. But more often they had trouble keeping up because most of them had never regularly attended school before. Father Flanagan saw that their needs were different than most children's.

With the help of the nuns, his niece and nephew, and the few other staff members he had hired, Father Flanagan devised his own schooling system. The parlors in the Home were transformed into classrooms, and the nuns added teaching to their already long list of duties. Father Flanagan also taught classes. An Omaha music teacher volunteered his services, and the Home assembled its first band.

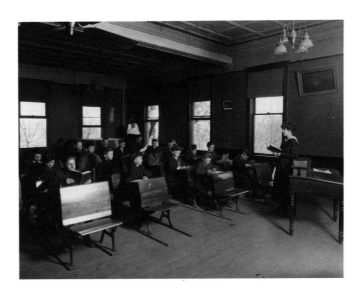

One of Father Flanagan's greatest desires was that every one of his boys would grow up to be an honest citizen, ". . . and it seems that the best method of insuring this is to teach him a trade at which he can earn an honest living." If the boys received an education and learned a trade, Father Flanagan was convinced they would leave the Home

A grade school classroom at the German-American Home.

with at least "two strikes in their favor." Based on this notion, the Home began its first trade school in the basement of the German-American Home.

Father Flanagan enlisted the services of "Mr. Joe," a retired shoemaker, to teach the boys the fine art of shoemaking and repairing. In the spring of 1919, Father Flanagan's Boys' Home created "The Sanitary Products Company." Soaps and disinfectants were produced by the boys in the basement and then sold to help make ends meet. Father Flanagan continued to hire staff to teach a wide variety of trades. The skills the boys learned would not only help them earn an "honest living" later, but benefited the Home as well. The shoe repair shop mended old shoes donated to the Home for the boys to wear; the bakery, which opened later, supplied bread and baked goods; the agricultural students raised vegetables and some livestock for the Home's food supply.

Still, it wasn't enough. More boys showed up on the doorstep daily, and Father Flanagan soon had no choice but to turn some away because he simply could not feed or house them all.

Overlook Farm

Father Flanagan needed additional space, a larger staff, and more supplies if he was to take in all the boys who needed his help. It was obvious that the Home needed more than one building and a garden plot in the backyard. In addition, many city residents had been uneasy with Flanagan's growing troupe of boys—ill-clothed, struggling educationally, and most controversial of all, racially and religiously mixed—living in the German-American Home. Many were critical of his Home, his boys, his methods. So Father Flanagan began to envision leaving Omaha for a much larger, open, and natural area—a place where there would be room to build, grow, and prosper, a good distance away from the protests of neighbors in the city.

Father Flanagan found what he was looking for ten miles west of Omaha. But the one-hundred-sixty-acre Overlook Farm was not for sale. Instead of looking

In the summer of 1921 six frame buildings were built on the farm to provide temporary living quarters and classroom space for the boys while a three hundred thousand dollar fund drive got underway to finance construction of a permanent building.

elsewhere, Father Flanagan insisted on talking with the owners, Anne Baum, her husband, David, and their daughter, Margaret. They were so moved by Father Flanagan's story that they agreed to sell. There was a small obstacle yet standing in Father Flanagan's way. He did not have nearly enough money to purchase the farm. The Baums accepted a forty-acre farm Father Flanagan had purchased earlier in trade, a small down payment and made arrangements for full payment later. They told Father Flanagan: "Your greatest business asset is your faith."

The purchase of Overlook Farm was only the beginning. While construction plans didn't include extravagances, the necessities alone for two hundred boys were overwhelming. They would need housing, a chapel, schoolrooms, a dining hall, and plenty of room for recreation. One thing Father Flanagan did not intend to build, however, was a fence. "This is a home," he explained to doubters who thought delinquent boys should be contained. "You do not wall in members of your family."

Before purchasing the farm, Father Flanagan had estimated that construction of a main building would cost three hundred thousand dollars and had already organized a fund-raising committee headed by J. E. Davidson, vice-president of Nebraska Power Company. Until the money was raised and the new building was completed, Father Flanagan and his boys would live and study in renovated barns and chicken coops and in temporary buildings hastily constructed by local workmen and the older boys.

Not even ten days after moving day in the fall of 1921 from the German-American Home, Father Flanagan began inviting the public to see the boys' new home. Each day he invited a group for lunch at the farm—the Kiwanis, the Omaha Women's Club, the Rotary Club. The boys guided their visitors on tours as Father Flanagan pointed out how new construction could help him care for five hundred boys instead of two hundred. Some of the boys served lunch while others entertained the guests by singing and performing musical selections on their second-hand instruments. These "delinquents" charmed their guests. Visitors agreed that the priest had a wonderful effect on these boys and supported his passion to touch the lives of hundreds more.

The Boys

"I shall be forever thankful that Father Flanagan took me in," said one of the boys in 1920. "He has given me the confidence that the world is not against me and other unfortunate boys."

Before he was ten, this boy had lost his father and watched his mother lose her struggle to support the family on her own. He eventually landed at the Home where he heard of even worse tragedies from the other boys.

"I thought I was the poorest boy in the world until I came to the Home and heard from other boys' lips of the hardships they had endured," he said. Hardships indeed. Newspaper headlines of the day read: "Poor Fear Cold, Give Tots Away;" (Parent) "'Pawns' Boy and Girl for $300;" "Hungry Children Faint in

Schools;" "Children Found Living with Pigs;" "Broken Homes Blamed for Erring Children;" "Nine Babies Abandoned Each Day in New York City."

Children were suffering in hundreds of ways, but their basic needs were the same. Father Flanagan knew that if left on the streets, boys like these would grow up to find themselves in jail—or worse. Most of the boys who had criminal records started by stealing food or snatching handbags to find money for a pair of shoes for the winter. Soon it became a way of life for them, a life Father Flanagan felt destined to change. "The youth who makes a mistake," Father Flanagan said, "may be compared to a plant growing in depleted soil and deprived of health-giving sunshine. He hasn't got a chance."

Gene Horan, a former resident and later a teacher at Boys Town, recalled one particular boy who thrived on the compassion and care he received at the Home. "One day a guy walked up to the grade school. He had the traditional knapsack on a stick. 'What're the chances of me wintering here?' he asked. Wintering meant that the carnival's traveling time was almost over and he needed a place to stay when the weather was cold. Well, he left that sack with the school principal and every spring he'd go back and ask, 'You still got my stuff? I might be leavin'.' But he stayed for six years, until he graduated."

The boys' gratitude for their home and for Father Flanagan's care was displayed by Ed, a student from Washington. One of Ed's fellow residents, Jim Mitchell, said, "They used to give graduating students here a suit and a few dollars in their pocket. When Ed came to the Home, he always told people, 'I came with nothing, so I'm going to leave with nothing.' After the graduation ceremony was over, he went back to his apartment, took off his suit, put it on a hanger, and told them to take it back to the tailor shop. He put on his jeans and shirt and left. He said, 'Father Flanagan educated me, fed me, took care of me, and that's all I could ever ask for.'"

Daily Life on the Farm

As soon as a boy reached the front steps of the Home—whether he was dropped there with a tag pinned to his clothes marked "Boys Town," wandered in on his own, or was sent by the courts—he fell into the daily routine followed by all the boys. He was awakened at 6:30 a.m. to allow him time to make his bed before breakfast.

"Idleness is the principle cause of delinquency," Father Flanagan said, so schoolwork and vocational training courses filled the day. Father Flanagan also saw that all the boys had free time to enjoy hobbies such as stamp collecting or model building. They could listen to the radio or play baseball, basketball, tops, or the boys' favorite—marbles. The boys were responsible for keeping their quarters clean and caring for the livestock and crops. The older boys even helped in completing the new buildings at Overlook Farm. The boys earned an allowance of twenty-five to forty cents for their chores. Most spent their earnings on candy, apples, or new marbles.

The farm was well-stocked with cattle, horses, pigs, calves, and chickens, and the boys soon learned to tend to their care.

One highlight for the boys was the weekly movie. A former employee remembers the event. "Sunday night was a very special time back in the old days. We would have dinner at five and the movie started at seven. They didn't want the little guys in the movie house early because they would get to jumping around. They were kind of a rambunctious group. So they would stand outside and as soon as they saw those doors open there would be a hundred little guys running across the field, just like a herd of buffalo."

The boys occasionally were treated to plays and musicals in town, shared holiday celebrations, and ate all their meals together, a practice Flanagan learned in the seminary. He insisted too that the boys say their nightly prayers together. But formal worship was always according to a boy's conscience. "Every boy must learn to pray," he said. "How he prays is up to him."

Boys of all creeds and some with no religion at all were at the Home. Boys were encouraged to continue practicing whatever faith they had learned before arriving at the Home. Catholic and Protestant services were held at the Home; Jewish boys were transported to synagogues in Omaha; and boys who had not received any religious guidance before were allowed to choose what religion they wanted to practice. They were constantly encouraged to pray, "for prayer can work miracles," Father Flanagan taught. "A true religious training for children is most essential if we are to expect to develop them into good men and good women—worthy citizens of our great country."

Another component to forming his boys into worthy citizens was teaching the boys about the law and government. Many knew much about the law—the wrong side of it. Father Flanagan let them experiment with self-government, holding elections for a mayor and a municipal court of students that helped enforce the Home's rules.

By the 1930s, life at Overlook Farm was stable and routine. With many more boys in his care, Father Flanagan now employed farm workers, telephone operators, secretaries, cooks, and housekeepers. A doctor stopped by daily for the boys' medical needs, and Creighton University dental students assisted an Omaha dentist once a week in cleaning and filling the boys' teeth. Father Flanagan had always handled admission applications to the Home himself, but the number of inquiries now exceeded his time, so a Welfare Department was formed.

One of the Home's many visitors commented: "I expected to see boys dressed alike and living under a sort of military discipline. I came here and found boys living in the atmosphere of a home, wearing clothes that they have brought with them or which have been supplied them, playing with their own tops or marbles, using baseball equipment that is community property, and laughing with a laughter that proves only one thing, happiness."

The Mothers' Guild

From the beginning, the good deeds of others had been crucial to the Home's survival and successes. In the early days, perhaps no group's contributions were more important than those of the Mothers' Guild. Originally, a group of women met at the Home on Thursday afternoons to sew quilts and mend clothing for the boys. Eventually the group took a more organized form under the leadership of Cassie Riley, meeting under the name of "The Mothers' Guild." Thursdays became known as "Mother's Day" at the Home.

The women were described in the *Boys' Home Journal* as "noble-hearted creatures of God leaving their own flock like the divine Master and coming down and spreading sunshine in the lives of the poor boys who have been deprived of their own dear mothers." Once officially organized in November 1920, the group

In the 1920s women gathered in Mothers' Clubs to make quilts and comforters, knit socks, and mend clothing for Father Flanagan's boys. By the end of the decade, there were Mothers' Clubs throughout the Midwest and as far away as New York.

not only continued to sew, but collected weekly dues of twenty-five cents. With their money, the Guild purchased Boy Scout uniforms and filled Christmas stockings.

Although the group was formed out of compassion for Father Flanagan's boys, the women enjoyed the social aspect of their club as well. "At their meeting the hostess makes a cake, or a box of doughnuts, or some other pastry that everyone likes," the *Journal* reported. "Sometimes they just have an afternoon party, have lunch and play cards or talk about their daily life, have a generally jolly time, collect the little fee charged and this money is sent to us by the secretary or treasurer."

Father Flanagan began receiving letters from women all over the country who wished to form clubs. Eventually the Mothers' Guild expanded to more than a dozen states, with groups formed as far away as New York.

An Empty Cupboard

While what would soon be known worldwide as "Boys Town" continued taking shape at Overlook Farm, Father Flanagan was busier than ever spreading the word of his home for boys so that he might save as many as he could from suffering and also gain financial backing. Although the campaign launched in the fall of 1921

In the summer of 1922 Father Flanagan's troupe of juvenile entertainers set off in three former circus wagons for a tour of Nebraska towns. The first wagon carried the boys, the second their beds, instruments, and a trunkful of toys, the third served as a kitchen complete with stove.

by Henry Monsky and other prominent Omaha businessmen had raised over two hundred thousand dollars for the construction of the main five-story building at the farm, the payment on the remaining mortgage still had to be met monthly, maintenance fees were escalating, and more boys were arriving at the Home each week. Father Flanagan's vision was still clear, his plans unchanged. He intended to keep his "City of Little Men" going regardless of cost.

Former resident and employee Al Witcofski said, "Father was a dreamer. He could sit and tell you what he was going to do two years from now, and it got done somehow."

As early as 1930 Father Flanagan began to talk and write about starting a "perpetual fund" built from public donations that would eventually be large enough to support the operation of the Home. Hard times during the Great Depression prevented him from actually opening such a fund until 1941. In the meantime, he struggled, sometimes from day to day, to keep the boys clothed and fed. Traveling to countless speaking engagements, pleading with citizens, organizing campaigns, and managing the Home's staff and finances, all while still making time for the boys, cost Father Flanagan his health. In August 1931 he was admitted to a Denver hospital specializing in respiratory problems. From his hospital bed, he made phone calls and wrote letters to friends and strangers asking for their help in paying the Home's debt.

In September 1931 he wrote: "Never in my life have I thought I would write such a letter as this. The Boys' Home for which I have worked so hard and for so many years, must be closed unless the necessary money is raised immediately.

". . . If the Home closes it will break my heart. That won't matter much. But it will break the hearts of these two hundred boys and deprive a chance in life to thousands of boys in the years to come. . . ."

Headlines in the *Boys' Home Journal* read: "$87,500 Must Be Raised at Once;" "Shall We Return These Homeless Boys to the Streets and Alleys?" "We Ask You Only for Financial Assistance in Order to Keep Our Doors Open." Drought and depression contributed to the struggle. In 1934 another headline read, "Our Cupboard Is Nearly Empty." The accompanying article pleaded, "Because we have no harvest, what our Home will use this year must be purchased. This means we must have money—money which must come from our friends, for we get no help from church, city, state, federal relief, or community chest."

Thousands of dollars did not pour in overnight, and at times the Home came perilously close to shutting its doors. Flanagan was forced to greatly reduce the number of boys by placing some on farms and in foster homes. Enough money came in each month, along with many small donations of food, clothing, and livestock, to feed and clothe the remaining boys and pay the mortgage. Slowly, the Home's financial footing improved, and the population of boys began to grow again. By 1936 the Home was stable enough to be incorporated as an official village in the state of Nebraska. In 1941 Father Flanagan was finally able to make the first deposit in his Foundation Fund. Boys Town was here to stay.

"He Ain't Heavy"

During the Home's early days Father Flanagan had used a photo of a young boy with arms outstretched to symbolize the "homeless boy" in his *Journal*, in mail appeals for funds, and on the first Boys Town seal. The photograph of Johnny Rushing had been taken by Louis R. Bostwick, a well-known Omaha photographer.

Bostwick had taken another photograph in the 1920s of two other boys—Howard Loomis being carried on the back of Reuben Granger. At the age of thirteen, Granger was brought to the German-American home and left by a woman assumed to be his mother. Granger later changed his name to Jim Edwards, saying he had no memory of or loyalty to his family which had abandoned him. He revisited Boys Town in 1991, for the first time in seventy years. He remembered Howard Loomis, who wore a leg brace and sometimes had trouble getting around. One day Father Flanagan took the boys to the Missouri River for a swim. Loomis was upset at the prospect of being left behind on the long, difficult walk to the river. "So I just picked him up, threw him on my back and away we went," said Edwards.

Inspiration for Boys Town's famous "Two Brothers" symbol may date as far back as this August 16, 1921, photograph of one of the Home's residents, Howard Loomis, being carried by another boy, Reuben Granger.

Years later, Father Flanagan saw an illustration of two boys in a similar pose in a 1941 Louis Allis Company publication, the *Messenger*, with the inscription, "He ain't heavy, Mr., he's m' brother." The illustration apparently reminded him of Loomis and Granger in Bostwick's photograph, for he requested the company's permission to adapt the illustration and phrase for Boys Town's use. Thereafter the trademarked "Two Brothers" and "He ain't heavy, Father. . . he's m' brother" became universally recognized symbols of Boys Town. And since 1949 millions of Americans have received Two Brothers seals from Boys Town and used them on their Christmas holiday mail.

"Boys Town" the Movie

Ever in search of an interesting story to tell on the screen, intrigued Hollywood producers in 1938 found their way to Boys Town, the subject of many newspaper and magazine articles. Father Flanagan was reluctant at first to have the story of Boys Town told Hollywood-style, fearful that the portrayal of his boys and his mission would not be accurate. MGM Studios President Louis B. Mayer assured him the movie MGM was planning would be true-to-life, finally convincing Father Flanagan to agree to the filming.

By June 1938 Spencer Tracy, Mickey Rooney, and a sixty-one-member crew headed by Director Norman Taurog arrived at Boys Town. They completed on-location filming in ten days. The boys were included, performing as extras in the film and helping prepare a farewell barbecue for the cast and crew. The film was finished quickly but was shelved for a month back in Hollywood because, Mayer was convinced, "It will never sell, there's no sex."

Urged by the cast and crew to release the film, Mayer agreed to an Omaha premiere on September 7, 1938. Although only one hundred fifty lucky citizens held tickets for the showing, a crowd of thirty thousand jammed the streets outside the Omaha Theatre—some peering from rooftops and telephone poles—to catch a glimpse of Tracy, Rooney, and other Hollywood stars who attended.

Omahans weren't the only ones impressed with the film. Newspapers across the country printed reports of people standing in line for hours to see "Boys Town." They emerged from the theaters sobbing, only to get back in line to see the second show. "Boys Town" won two Academy Awards. Dore Schary and Eleanore Griffin were honored for writing the Best Original Screenplay and Spencer Tracy won the Best Actor award for his portrayal of Father Flanagan. Truly in the spirit of Father Flanagan, Tracy graciously accepted the Oscar only to give it to Boys Town, where it remains on display today.

Director Norman Taurog, seated and wearing an African pith helmet, supervised the on-location filming of "Boys Town." Oppressive heat and humidity took its toll on cast and crew.

Fame

Famous visitors such as Babe Ruth, Lou Gehrig, Franklin Roosevelt, and Tom Mix had found their way to the Home as early as 1927. The movie only increased the Home's spreading recognition and popularity. "Boys Town" became and remained a household phrase. Boys Town, Father Flanagan, and his famous "There is no such thing as a bad boy," became familiar references in popular culture, continuing into the 1990s in the "Superman" movie series and in TV shows such as "Cheers" and "Night Court."

In the 1930s and '40s, civic clubs and leaders clamored for Father Flanagan to

After the movie's release, Father Flanagan traveled and made speeches tirelessly. In August 1941 he spoke at Broadmoor Stadium in Colorado Springs, Colorado.

give advice and speak on the welfare of America's children. Spurred by the movie's success, Bing Crosby, Bob Hope, George Burns and Gracie Allen, as well as a parade of other entertainers, sports figures, and politicians that continued over the years were welcomed at the Home. Visits from these celebrities proved not only exciting for the boys, but sometimes profitable.

"We didn't have any baseball uniforms then. We played in our overalls," Al Witcofski recalled. "Until two comedians came. Bud Abbott and Lou Costello. They bought the uniforms. That's the way we got pretty near everything. Somebody would always come through."

Father Flanagan agreed to as many speaking engagements as he could, but requests came from all across the country. The hundreds of speeches Father Flanagan gave to organizations—from local clubs to the U.S. Senate—were often titled, "Juvenile Delinquency," "Need for Christian Love in Dealing with Young People," and perhaps his most famous, "There's No Such Thing as a Bad Boy." (This last phrase was coined by Floyd Starr of Starr Commonwealth Schools, Inc., but was so popularized by Father Flanagan that it became known as his own.)

Father Flanagan's knowledge was much sought after. In 1941 he was called upon by the governor of California and Judge Benjamin Lindsay to devise a new program for Whittier State School, where two young residents had committed suicide and there were reported incidents of severe abuse of children.

Father Flanagan's enervating pace proved, once again, detrimental to his health, but he pushed on. His ever-present respiratory problems flared several times, sending him to hospitals. Once reasonably healthy again, Father Flanagan continued his work with even more fervor.

Father Flanagan in Chicago to raise money for the war effort. By November 1942 he had helped sell three million dollars in U.S. War Bonds.

World War II had begun and had called thousands of fathers away from their families. Father Flanagan recognized that many children were suffering in single-parent homes. Some had to quit going to school to help their mothers support large families; some went hungry; others were forced to leave their homes to be cared for despite every effort to keep them there. He spoke to groups frequently about the conditions of these children. He also went on war bond tours, selling three million dollars in bonds in 1942.

Secretary of War Robert Patterson and Gen. Douglas MacArthur requested that Father Flanagan examine the conditions of war orphans in Japan and Korea in 1947. He made the trip and subsequently reported his recommendations to President Harry S Truman.

Losing a Friend

In 1948, again at the request of the War Department, Father Flanagan traveled to Europe for the same purpose. In Berlin, Germany, on May 15 Father Flanagan suffered a heart attack. Both a priest and a doctor came to his bedside, along with his nephew Patrick Norton who had made the trip with him. Norton recalled:

> While Father (Emmitt) Walsh (an Army chaplain) said the prayers for the dead, Father, in his characteristic manner, stroked his bushy eyebrow. As the prayers were finished, Father Flanagan himself concluded the prayer with "Amen." It was his last word. Father Flanagan was dead. It was a beautiful death, if death can be called beautiful.

Across the ocean, as Father Flanagan's boys sat listening to a radio program, the shocking news came over the air waves.

> We interrupt this program to bring you a bulletin from Berlin, Germany. Father Flanagan, founder and director of the famed Boys Town, Nebraska, died suddenly this morning.

Within minutes of the special broadcast, the boys solemnly filled Dowd Memorial Chapel. For the first time in thirty-one years, homeless boys wondered who would care for them. Telegrams poured in from around the world. Expressing their sorrow were Harry Truman, J. Edgar Hoover, Spencer Tracy, Frank Leahy, John Considine, Jr., Norman Taurog, and hundreds of others. President Truman wired:

> American youth and youth everywhere have lost an ever faithful friend in the untimely death of Father Flanagan. His unshaken confidence in the love of God and in even the least of God's children found eloquent expression in the declaration that there is no such thing as a bad boy. He has left a living monument in the countless boys who are today honest men and upright citizens because of his benign influence and abiding faith in the inherent goodness of human nature.

Charles Kenworthy, who had grown up at the Home, wrote, "Words cannot express my sorrow at the loss of the man who raised me."

B'nai B'rith, which had only one year earlier lost its president, Henry Monsky, to a heart attack at the age of fifty-seven, wired: "His warm friendship for and common interest with our late President Monsky exemplified (the) spirit of brotherhood which we fervently hope will someday encompass all

Soon after Father Flanagan's death on May 15, 1948, a crowd at Municipal Field awaited the military plane bearing his body back from Berlin. U.S. Air Force Photograph

Army personnel and Boys Town seniors who served as pallbearers escorted Father Flanagan's coffin from the aircraft.

peoples. Your loss is ours as well."

Spencer Tracy hoped "the memory of a man as great as he will help sustain (the boys) in their sorrow for he was truly a fine, a good, man." From Notre Dame University, Football Coach Frank Leahy wrote, "His marvelous influence and tremendous inspiration could not be measured and will continue to guide each of us who had the privilege of knowing him." J. Edgar Hoover said "we of the FBI consider this a personal loss."

In a May 16th broadcast, radio commentator Drew Pearson said, "It was Father Flanagan's firm conviction that there is no such thing as a bad boy. All over this land there are graduates of Boys Town who owe their place in society to Father Flanagan. His hand was extended to any boy who needed him, regardless of color or creed. No matter how forsaken or discouraged or defiant a boy, Father Flanagan could reach him. His Boys Town was a workshop where he molded character, bolstered self-confidence, distilled new hope for the future. The world is poorer for the loss of Father Flanagan, but we are all richer for having felt the influence of a man who by living democracy made democracy live."

Three days after his death, Father Flanagan's mortal remains were returned to his beloved Boys Town. A crowd of fifteen hundred met the military airplane. Father Flanagan's prized Boys Town Band stood mute as bugler Frank Lyons sounded "Taps."

The *Boys Town Times* reported that an estimated thirty thousand people viewed Father Flanagan's body as it lay in state two days prior to burial. "Omaha paid final tribute to Father Flanagan as city, county and business suspended activities the morning of the funeral."

On May 21, 1948, Rev. Edmond C. Walsh was the celebrant for the first funeral Mass held for citizens of Boys Town, alumni, relatives, and staff members. Rev. Mr. Ben Martin served as the master of ceremonies, while Rev. Leo Kuhn and Rev. John Farrald served as deacon and subdeacon. Their service to the church itself was a tribute to Father Flanagan, as all three were graduates of Boys Town. A public Solemn Mass of Requiem followed. Father Flanagan's brother, Rev. P. A. Flanagan, was the celebrant.

Father Flanagan was laid to his final rest in the Baptistry of Dowd Memorial Chapel. The marble slab that sealed the sarcophagus read: "Father Flanagan, Founder of Boys Town, Lover of Christ and Man. July 13, 1886 – May 15, 1948"

Boys Town students filed past Father Flanagan's bier before the funeral Mass on May 21, 1948, in Dowd Chapel.

Monsignor Nicholas H. Wegner, executive director of Boys Town from 1948 to 1973.

"Who Will Care For Us Now?"

In 1946 a priest in his early thirties from South Omaha who had served in the war as a Navy Chaplain, Father Edmond Walsh, was assigned by Omaha Archbishop James Hugh Ryan to work at Boys Town. During the ensuing two years, the relationship between Flanagan and Walsh became a close one. Perhaps with some premonition, Father Flanagan mentioned publicly, on the eve of his trip to Germany, that Walsh was his choice to succeed him as executive director of Boys Town. Indeed, Father Walsh was named acting director immediately following Father Flanagan's death.

Archbishop Ryan, however, had died several months before Father Flanagan. And in the summer and early fall of 1948, circumstances in the Archbishop's office caused events at Boys Town to take a different direction. In September the new Archbishop Gerald T. Bergan named Monsignor Nicholas H. Wegner as Boys Town's second executive director. No public reason for the decision was ever given. However, it is likely that Archbishop Bergan wished to name his own man as diocesan chancellor, a post Monsignor Wegner had held since 1939, and appointing Wegner to the Boys Town position allowed him to do that.

Wegner was born in 1898, the eleventh of twelve children in a Nebraska farm family. As a teenage pitching sensation he played semi-professional baseball for several teams. Wegner saved his fifty to one hundred dollar game pay to cover his tuition at St. Joseph's Seminary in Illinois, eventually turning down several offers to play major league baseball. He went on to study in Rome and was ordained in that city on March 7, 1925. Returning to Omaha, Father Wegner's first assignment was as assistant pastor of St. Cecilia's Cathedral. In 1929 he was appointed assistant chancellor and as an able administrator, began his steady rise through the ranks within the Omaha diocese.

Whatever Archbishop Bergan's reason for Wegner's assignment to lead Boys Town, the surprise appointment and Father Walsh's crushing disappointment made for a traumatic transition period. Monsignor Wegner reassured the staff and the public that he had closely followed and supported Father Flanagan's work. He quickly tried to calm those who feared radical change at the Home:

> In the administration of Boys Town I will try in every way possible to follow in the footsteps of its founder. And while I look with a great deal of fear and trepidation to the task that lies before me, I feel that with the help and the cooperation of the very able staff at Boys Town and the help of God and the prayer of our friends, the good work so ably begun by Father Flanagan and carried to such glorious heights will continue to prosper and meet with success. . .

True to his word, Monsignor Wegner did employ Father Flanagan's philosophies in running the Home. When Boys Town's tolerance for racial and religious differences was challenged, Monsignor Wegner responded to critics by simply saying, "Admission to Boys Town is based primarily upon the boy's need for a home." Later, under attack for allowing religious differences, he wrote:

Although Father Flanagan's Boys' Home was founded by a Catholic priest, please be advised that we accept boys regardless of their creed or color. . . . No boy under our care is obligated in any way, shape or form to become a Catholic, and we have a Protestant minister who conducts Protestant services for the boys of the various Protestant affiliations.

Expansion and Security

Monsignor Wegner, however, wanted to do more than defend the philosophies of his predecessor. Not only did he intend to maintain the existing programs, he aspired to double the Home's population by acting on Father Flanagan's earlier expansion plans. He also intended to attain financial security for the Home in keeping with Father Flanagan's intentions.

Father Flanagan had set campus expansion plans in motion before his death, and Monsignor Wegner spent most of his first year seeing them through. The

The Field House was built during the 1948 expansion and in 1978 named for longtime coach Skip Palrang. Nativity Protestant Chapel was added to the building in 1953. Before the chapel was built, Protestant services were held in a classroom.

building plan that Father Flanagan had devised in 1946 was completed during Monsignor Wegner's first year as director. A new high school, dining hall, twelve-hundred-seat music hall, vocational career center, field house, and twenty-five new cottages were spread across the expanding campus. From a waiting list of three thousand, Monsignor Wegner took in approximately fifty additional boys each month. The best research indicates that the Home's population peaked at eight hundred eighty in the 1960s. In addition to Father Flanagan's expansion plans, a Protestant chapel, a forty-bed hospital and clinic, an orientation center and, later, a middle school were built on the burgeoning campus.

Monsignor Wegner's second goal of financial security seemed further out of reach. Father Flanagan's expansion plans alone left a debt of six million dollars. Father Flanagan had said, "Divine Providence will take care of that. . . ." when asked how he planned to repay the debt. Flanagan, however, proved to be as visionary in his pioneering fund-raising techniques as he had been in the care of abandoned and troubled boys. In the late 1930s the Home began to apply mass mailing techniques to what had been basically a regional fund-raising effort. Flanagan hired a financial director and Boys Town started purchasing mailing lists and sending appeal letters to potential donors nationwide at Christmas and Easter. Continuing this practice, Monsignor Wegner hoped to repay the Home's debts and build the endowment fund to eventually eliminate or partially eliminate the need to appeal for support. Father Flanagan's popularity had grown to be worldwide, and even after his death more and more people continued to be generous to his boys and his Home.

Champions

Monsignor Wegner's guidance helped the boys gain a reputation of excellence in many extracurricular activities. The Boys Town "Aggies" 4-H Club produced Grand National Champion livestock and often entered them at fairs and expositions. In 1949 the club began hosting the Boys Town Royal Livestock Show at the Field House every August for 4-H clubs from throughout the Midwest.

Under the direction of Father Francis Schmitt, the Boys Town Choir became known nationwide. The choir was heard on radio and television and made annual tours that took them to cities across the United States, Japan, Canada, and Cuba. Carnegie Hall, President Truman, Ed Sullivan, and Disney World all hosted the famous group. The Boys Town Choir recorded albums of Christmas music with the Everly Brothers in 1962 and with Gordon MacRae in 1978.

Monsignor Wegner was an avid sportsman, pitching baseball throughout his college years and turning down two major league contracts to become a priest. He and Coach Maurice "Skip" Palrang, twice named Pop Warner Coach of the Year, did much to create outstanding athletic traditions at Boys Town. Boys Town chalked up victory after victory, including several state championships, in football, swimming, basketball, baseball, track, and wrestling. Many of Boys Town's outstanding young athletes ventured out and made their mark in amateur and professional sports after graduation.

The Boys Town Cowboys football team didn't join the Omaha Metropolitan League until 1964. Before then, the team played exhibition games in twenty-one states and Washington, D.C., before crowds of as many as forty thousand spectators. The team traveled across the country in the "Flex," the team bus nicknamed by the boys. The "Flex" became part of the great athletic tradition as it carried team after championship team to opponents' schools for twenty-two years. Team members often demanded that the driver travel

Monsignor Wegner umpiring a game with Aloysius Steinbock at bat. A talented baseball pitcher, Wegner had turned down contract offers in 1915 to play major league ball with the Cleveland Indians and the St. Louis Browns in order to remain in the seminary and pursue his training for the priesthood. When this photograph was taken, Wegner explained that he held up a three-fingered strike sign to indicate that boys always had another chance at Boys Town.

particular highway routes to guarantee victory and not "jinx" a winning streak.

While the boys excelled in extracurricular activities, Monsignor Wegner

certainly didn't let them ignore their priorities at school, church, and home. He tried to make sure that each boy left the Home with a marketable skill. The Vocational Career Center offered courses in tailoring, barbering, auto mechanics, ceramics, and industrial arts. The boys were each managers of their own student bank accounts. The Home established a scholarship fund so that those students who wished to enroll in a university or post-secondary training school would have the opportunity.

The new Vocational Career Center provided the boys with an expanded curriculum, facilities, and equipment. Auto mechanics and electronics were two of the courses offered.

At home in their cottages, the older boys had equal responsibilities for chores and schoolwork. Not unlike Father Flanagan's first boys, they were allowed ample time for television or game playing after homework assignments were completed.

Monsignor Wegner believed children needed to learn the lessons of worship, reverence, good will, and moral responsibility that religion could teach. He encouraged personal and social religious habits in the boys, such as prayer and regular church or synagogue attendance. Above all, Monsignor Wegner instilled in the hearts of his boys the importance of being their "brother's keeper."

Changing Times

In late 1959 Monsignor Wegner checked into the Mayo Clinic in Rochester, Minnesota, for stomach surgery. After the procedure, he developed a staph infection from which he did not recover for six months. Monsignor Wegner returned to work part-time in April 1960, but in the next fifteen years he underwent surgery another fourteen times for various ailments and generally suffered from declining health.

At the same time Monsignor Wegner was struggling with health problems, Boys Town was being presented with more difficult challenges. In the turbulent counterculture and antiwar years of the late 1960s and early 1970s, youth started to arrive at Boys Town with histories of drug problems, suicide attempts, physical battering, and sexual abuse. For too many children the "Age of Aquarius" led to drug and alcohol addiction. The antiwar movement was too often just a pretext for kids to shake their fists at authority—parents, teachers, adults in general. Father Flanagan's tried-and-true treatment methods—love, shelter, and vocational training—were not geared to deal with these problems. And as Boys Town looked around the country, no one else knew how to help these children either.

New treatment technologies were needed to help children overcome the devastating effects of drugs and abuse in their family life. Boys Town was approaching a crossroads. It would soon have to choose between sticking with the familiar, comfortable methods of the past that no longer worked or taking the major risk of searching for a way to really change the behavior of troubled children.

The Endowment Fund

In his deliberate and conservative manner, Monsignor Wegner had been working on the Home's finances. He was successful in soliciting funds both for operations and to build the endowment fund. As a private institution, however, Boys Town had never been required to report publicly on the size of this fund. Through most of Monsignor Wegner's tenure that was standard practice: Private institutions remained private, especially regarding their finances. By the early 1970s, however, there was a new outlook: Private institutions offering public service should be subject to public scrutiny of their finances.

On March 30, 1972, the *Omaha Sun* newspapers published a story on Boys Town's finances. It could have been a simple facts-and-figures story stating that Boys Town's Foundation Fund was worth over one hundred and fifty million dollars and that its net worth, adding the value of buildings and grounds, was over two hundred million dollars. These were the days of Watergate, however, with traditional institutions under attack. Under big headlines, the *Sun* played the story as an exposé, and wire services spread it from coast to coast.

As details of the story became known, however, another viewpoint emerged. A columnist for the *New York News* commented, "There is no scandal in the Boys Town operation; they are just successful at what they do, and the money is going to good use."

Boys Town officials explained that nearly all other institutions such as schools, universities, libraries, and hospitals "almost from necessity" create endowment programs to augment their income from tuition, fees, and contributions. Many also conduct frequent capital fund-raising campaigns.

Most of the money in Boys Town's endowment fund had been set aside as private memorials from wills and estates, not from the mail appeals which had been used to pay annual operating costs. The Board acknowledged that the Home had made emotional direct mail appeals for money while not acknowledging the size of the Foundation Fund. And the 1972 Christmas mail appeal was cancelled.

However, Monsignor Wegner explained, "There were times in the early days when this Home was on the point of closing because of lack of funds." Because of its endowment fund, "Boys Town will be here for years to come, binding up the hurts of children and teenage youth and setting them on the road to good citizenship. . . ."

Board member Arthur W. Knapp said, "You have to keep perpetuating yourself. (Boys Town) is something that has caught hold of the average man, who wants to feel he is part of helping something that is really great."

National Study

Even before the *Omaha Sun* articles were published, the Board of Trustees had decided to hire a consulting firm to undertake a major evaluation of the Home's youth care program and financial situation. The firm hired, Booz, Allen and Hamilton Inc., completed a multi-volume study that recommended a number of things: It urged Boys Town to expand its programs and services into new areas and to continue raising funds. It also recommended that the Home make a sweeping change in its system of youth care. The study outlined the societal changes that made group care of the boys in dormitory settings outdated and ineffective. Several approaches that offered more individualized care of children were proposed as alternatives.

After considering the consultants' recommendations, in June 1972 the Home announced that an Institute for the Study and Treatment of Hearing and Speech Disorders in Children had been approved by the Board at a cost of thirty million dollars. A few months later, the Board gave preliminary approval to a forty million dollar program for the study of youth development. In addition, the Home began a practice of releasing and publishing its financial information in an annual report made available to the public and press in early spring.

The Boys Town National Research Hospital (BTNRH), originally named the Boys Town Institute, treats thousands of youngsters with hearing and speech problems annually.

A Change at the Helm

These changes did not go far enough, however. The Board also needed to address the way Boys Town was taking care of its children on the Home Campus. The current program was neither changing the behavior of the children nor coping with the onslaught of problems brought about by rampant drug use and rising child abuse. The task of searching for and implementing a new childcare technology, the Board felt, was too demanding for Monsignor Wegner, now seventy-five years old and in poor health. He did not want to leave the helm at Boys Town after twenty-five years of service, but on September 15, 1973, against his wishes, Monsignor Wegner retired. He continued to reside on campus in living quarters at the clinic until a series of strokes in 1975 sent him to St. Catherine's Hospital Center for Continuing Care. There, on March 18, 1976, he died. His funeral services were held in Dowd Chapel on the Boys Town campus. In 1977 Boys Town's middle school was named in his honor.

Of Monsignor Wegner, the *Omaha World-Herald* commented, "He had to take on the mantle of Father Flanagan as the shepherd of Boys Town. It was a tough act to follow. It didn't take long to find out that Boys Town was in good hands. What Father Flanagan planted, Monsignor Wegner brought to full flower. Boys Town today, in its security and continuity, is as much a monument to Monsignor Wegner's dedication and singleness of purpose as it is to Father Flanagan's vision."

Monsignor Wegner and boys at his retirement dinner in the Grade School Dining Hall on September 10, 1973.

Father Robert P. Hupp, executive director of Boys Town from 1973 to 1985.

"On the Shoulders of Giants"

The man to whom Archbishop Daniel Sheehan and the Board turned to guide Boys Town through the challenging, even risky, years of change ahead was the Rev. Robert P. Hupp. Hupp, a native Nebraskan, was born on July 3, 1915, the oldest of nine children. He studied at St. Louis Preparatory Seminary and Kenrick Seminary (where he was known as "The Clipper" because he cut his classmates' hair to earn tuition money). After being ordained into the priesthood at St. Cecilia's Cathedral in Omaha in 1940, he served at two Omaha parishes, then as a chaplain in the United States Navy during World War II. Later, Father Hupp founded Christ the King parish and became Vicar General of the Archdiocese of Omaha. He became the third executive director of Boys Town on October 11, 1973.

"In 1973, when I came upon the scene, it was no great feat to move ahead. We see far, you know, when we stand on the shoulders of giants. It was the charismatic program innovator, Father Flanagan, complemented by the administrative executive, Monsignor Wegner, who provided the frame for me to climb," said Father Hupp, several years later.

The Search

The youth of the 1970s were in many ways very different from the first boys Father Flanagan rescued from the streets and alleys of Omaha. Few of the boys at the home were now orphans in the sense that they had no living parents; rather they were what Father Hupp referred to as "social orphans." For many of them, family life had been eroded by abuse, poverty, drugs, alcoholism, or divorce. Children now arrived at Boys Town with severe emotional and behavioral troubles. These problems, the Board felt, dictated a different childcare approach than the one Boys Town had been using with few changes since its founding. The

With family-style living instituted on campus, the boys shared meals with their Family-Teachers in the home rather than in large dining halls.

search for a new approach to help these troubled children was long and arduous, marked by false starts, disappointing results, and new beginnings.

One of the many alternative approaches to youth care offered in the Booz, Allen and Hamilton study and investigation was a family-style setting. Father Hupp and a screening committee from the Board of Trustees undertook a national search for a director of youth care who could implement a "family concept" in the treatment of Boys Town residents.

The search for a "family concept" culminated with adoption of the Teaching-Family Model from Achievement Place at Kansas University in Lawrence, Kansas. The Teaching-Family Model grew out of a research/funding collaboration between

Family-Teacher Sylvester
Wilson helped several boys
with their homework.

the Bureau of Child Research at Lawrence, Kansas, and the National Institute of Mental Health's Center for Crime and Delinquency. The primary objectives of the Teaching-Family Model had been to develop a community-based, family-style, skill-oriented group home treatment for disadvantaged and delinquent youth that was effective, economical, satisfactory to its consumers, and replicable by other programs. Boys Town was attracted by the careful research and development that had gone into this program. Proponents of the Teaching-Family Model thought that it was impossible to put the model in place at a large "institution" such as Boys Town. Many argued that the Home Campus should be abandoned and homes only put into the community. Boys Town insisted, however, that it could make a unique contribution and further adapt the model. So it was decided to hire a number of Achievement Place staff members to adopt and refine the program in as many as fifty homes on the Home Campus.

In late 1974 four couples moved into four of the former cottages and turned them into "homes." These couples helped other staff members put together a training manual. As soon as other couples were trained, they moved into the remaining cottages and sixteen newly built homes. The last of the dormitories closed and the transition to family homes at Boys Town was complete by the end of 1975.

In hindsight it is easy to say that Boys Town searched for and found this "Teaching-Family Model," developing it through the years with such success. The reality was far more difficult, far more uncertain day to day, and far less clear in design and execution. Father Hupp was determined to change Boys Town to meet the needs of the time, and there is nothing more difficult to accomplish than radical organizational change. There were, for a long time, more people opposed to the changes than in favor of them. There were also some false starts. For example, Boys Town's support for three research centers was ended in the early 1980s because the general studies of youth development being done were not program-related and did not help the Home develop better ways of taking care of its children.

The Families of Boys Town

Under the new youth care system installed by Father Hupp and his staff, each home on campus housed eight to ten boys of all ages and ethnic backgrounds. With them lived "Family-Teachers," a highly trained and carefully selected husband and wife who cared for the children day in and day out. Their sole responsibility was for the love, care, and treatment of the boys in their home. They lived in the homes twenty-four hours a day.

The Boys Town youth care system is a skills deficit model. The childcare technology that was developed on campus and practiced in the homes includes these elements:

Family-Teachers use a specific *teaching* procedure with the youths for correcting inappropriate behavior and encouraging positive behavior. Family-Teachers foster the youths' *relationship development* by modeling how to be cooperative, helpful, and positive and to treat others with sensitivity and respect. Each home runs on a *self-government* system where youths can participate in decisions and rule-making at family meetings. Depending on each youth's development and behavior, a more- or less-structured *motivation system* is used. Throughout each day a youth earns or loses "points" and ultimately privileges such as using the telephone, watching TV, etc., based on his behavior. This point system is eventually phased out as the youth internalizes his behavior and takes responsibility for individual actions in positive, constructive ways.

Essential to Boys Town's program and what make it successful are four components: First, each married couple receives *training* that begins even before they move into the home and literally never ends. Couples begin training by living in on-campus apartments, observing experienced couples in various childcare and home operation activities, and attending a three-week Preservice Workshop. About half of the workshop is spent role-playing or practicing the skills they will need in caring for the youth and operating their home. Training continues all through the career of Family-Teachers—it is a way of life. Elementary behavior-shaping skills provide a base for ongoing advanced skill-based training.

Once in the home, Family-Teachers receive *consultation* services from an administrative staff member who offers advice and support, helps during crises, observes them at work, and provides continuing in-service training. Consultants are usually former certified Family-Teachers who receive special training in consultation skills and serve an apprenticeship period with an experienced Consultant. Consultants work with Family-Teachers before and during their move into a home. They are available twenty-four hours a day either by phone or in person. Consultants often observe and give feedback on the Family-Teachers' work in the homes, regularly reviewing each child's progress and helping the couple develop treatment plans. As an important guiding member of the treatment team, Consultants help Family-Teachers develop sound professional skills and maintain their enthusiasm, concern, and objectivity.

Activity in one of the new homes for girls on campus. When asked by Father Hupp, the first girls at the Home said they overwhelmingly supported leaving the "Boys Town" name intact despite the addition of girls to the population.

Third, an *evaluation* system assures accountability and the highest level of treatment success possible. The youth, the youth's parents or guardian, teachers and principal, probation officer, and judge are all asked to rate and comment on the services provided by the Family-Teachers. A steady flow of other information about activities in each home comes in throughout the year and contributes to the evaluation process. All the evaluation information is used to determine whether or not a couple will become "certified" Family-Teachers. A couple that fails to pass their first evaluation is given a second, final chance usually within thirty days. These evaluations take place annually. Certification means that Family-Teachers have consistently provided a safe, loving family environment, that their children like and respect them, and that each child is learning important skills and values.

Finally, Boys Town designed its *administrative systems* to meet the needs of its boys and girls living in a family-style environment, and not vice versa. Administrative procedures ease the burden of Family-Teachers and facilitate the accomplishment of treatment goals for each youth. Administration provides supervision (community directors) and support services (an assistant, home checking account, etc.) for Family-Teachers. It also establishes policies and procedures in program areas such as admissions, staff recruitment and training, licensing, and budgets.

Religious education and practice have been part of Boys Town's foundation since the days of Father Flanagan. Religious development now became a responsibility of the home as well as the church and school. Family-Teachers were and are asked to respect and enhance the religious traditions of Boys Town youth without proselytizing. They attend church with the youth, teach proper church behavior, model and teach religious home habits such as prayer, reflection, and study.

The transition at Boys Town was slow, sometimes painful, but ultimately invigorating for the organization and healing for the youth. For many of the boys admitted to Boys Town, it was their first experience with a family that didn't yell or hit each other, had two parents who cared about them, had rules, and most important, a family that never gave up on them.

"Even though we're not family in blood," said one student, "we are a family through God, peace, and happiness."

Extending the Boys Town Family

"We must never be content to stand still when children are at risk," Father Hupp said. It was obvious that the number of children needing long-term care was far greater than what Boys Town could treat on its campus. In 1975 Father Hupp decided to offer Boys Town's system of youth care to other organizations. The Community-Based Systems Program (later called the Boys Town National Group Home Program) was formed to provide training and technical assistance to group homes owned by other agencies. By the mid-1980s, more than ninety affiliated family homes in thirteen states were using the Boys Town childcare technology.

Boys Town's Hospital

Gradual but steady progress had taken place in developing the Boys Town Institute for Communication Disorders since its approval under Monsignor Wegner's administration. A new facility had been built in downtown Omaha that incorporated bright colors, wall murals, play areas, and special child-level windows to make children's visits to the hospital more enjoyable. By 1977 the highly trained team of physicians and technicians moved into the specialized facility.

Researchers had found that childhood communication disorders were an important element in educational, social, and emotional problems. Through diagnosis, treatment, and study of speech, hearing, language, and learning problems, the Boys Town Institute hoped to improve the futures of communicatively handicapped children. The Institute's name was changed in 1989 to the Boys Town National Research Hospital (BTNRH) as the hospital gained a national reputation as a referral center for children with communication disorders.

In response to the special needs of communicatively handicapped children, the hospital developed new programs. Testing of deaf students revealed that many of those with superior nonverbal IQs were not succeeding in school or participating in activities. A summer program on the Boys Town campus was initiated in 1980 with academics, physical and fine arts, and social and computer activities to stimulate such gifted hearing-impaired teenagers.

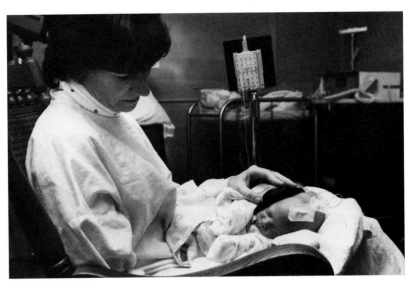

A hospital staff member administered an auditory brainstem response test that can detect the degree and type of hearing loss in an infant.

BTNRH was quickly at the forefront of technology and research. In 1983 researchers at the hospital discovered a defective gene that influences the reading disability, dyslexia. Hospital scientists also localized a gene for Usher's Syndrome Type II, a disease that causes both blindness and deafness in children. In 1991 the U.S. Department of Health and Human Services awarded BTNRH a three-year, five million dollar grant. BTNRH's application was ranked first in a field of twenty from leading institutions. Along with Johns Hopkins University and the University of Iowa, BTNRH was selected as one of the first three national research and training centers in communication disorders—the only one in the area of childhood deafness.

Alternative Education

In 1980 Boys Town and Father Hupp turned their attention to the critical needs of young people who end up on the streets after dropping out or being expelled from school—modern day equivalents to Father Flanagan's first street waifs. Since 1968 Dominican High School had been Omaha's alternative educational opportunity for students who had failed in other schools. But in 1979 these students were faced with losing this opportunity when the school was threatened with demolition to make room for a freeway.

Rather than see this school close and in keeping with Father Flanagan's ideals of educational opportunity for all youth, Father Hupp and the Boys Town Board

To help teenaged mothers stay in school, Flanagan High offers them the services of its child care center.

of Trustees responded to an appeal from a special committee and took over the program. The board authorized the construction of a new building to be called Father Flanagan High School. It would be built in the inner city to be accessible to the students and parents it was to serve.

The school opened in 1983 with a capacity for two hundred students, most of whom were high dropout risks from traditional high schools because of poverty, drug addiction, alcoholism, or teenage pregnancy. Flanagan High tailored its educational and social service programs to help these students complete school and improve their chances for employment and self-sufficiency. The school's program was accredited by the State of Nebraska and the North Central Association of Colleges and Schools. It offered students a complete high school curriculum, including religious education, career preparation, self-discipline skills, and parenting classes. In 1984 the school was honored by the United States Department of Education as an Exemplary Private School.

Girls on Campus

"I hadn't been at Boys Town for more than a week," recalled Father Hupp, "before I got a call from Juvenile Court Judge Colleen Buckley asking me when we would start taking girls. I told her to just give me time." The Boys Town Institute had been treating girls with communication disorders since its 1977 opening, but the residential care program was still limited to boys.

Father Hupp's experience working with girls (from 1946 to 1950 he served as chaplain, teacher, and athletics coach for a girls' home run by the Sisters of the Good Shepherd Convent in Omaha) and his awareness of their problems encouraged him to accept five girls into the Boys Town residential program in 1978. In what was thought would be a small and short-term experiment, those first girls lived in an off-campus downtown home that Boys Town owned. A few girls began living on campus in 1979 and their number reached a maximum of twenty-six by 1985.

"I saw it as an experimental program," said Father Hupp. "I also had trouble convincing the Board of Trustees that accepting girls wasn't a mistake. But when the girls arrived, it actually improved the behavior of the boys."

The small number of girls caused little stir on campus, but a much greater commotion among alumni and the general public. The media began bombarding Father Hupp with questions. Was he going to change Boys Town's name? What did he think about "People Town?" Father Hupp called a meeting with the girls on campus and asked what they thought. Their unanimous answer: "We want to live at *Boys* Town."

Boys Town USA

The residential care program developed at Boys Town had four characteristics by the early 1980s: It was *safe*. Children were truly free from the fear of abandonment and abuse. The treatment was *effective*; kids actually got better. The treatment was *family-centered*, and the children were *happy* to be at Boys Town. The question at this time became: Was the program *replicable* and exportable to other sites? Father Hupp had received many requests from communities around the country "to start another Boys Town." In addition, he had become increasingly concerned about other childcare agencies affiliating with the National Group Home Program, using Boys Town's name, but not fully adopting the Boys Town program. So in 1983 he announced the development of a new program called Boys Town USA that would establish childcare sites around the country, with residential care homes that would be wholly-owned and operated by Boys Town.

In 1984 the first Boys Town home outside of Nebraska was opened in Tallahassee, Florida. This single dwelling with six boys was the first step in a process to see if Boys Town could deliver the same high-quality care of children away from the Home Campus.

Father Flanagan Service Award

A new tradition began in 1975 to honor and recognize others from around the world who shared Father Flanagan's philosophy of saving children from lives of despair by serving their interests in many different ways. That year Boys Town awarded the first Father Flanagan Award for Service to Youth to Mrs. Spencer Tracy for her work with hearing-impaired children. Other winners followed: Mother Teresa (1976), Bob Hope (1977), Dr. Mildred Jefferson (1978), Dr. Jonas Salk (1979), Robert and Dorothy DeBolt (1980), Danny Thomas (1981), Julius Erving (1984), Don Keough (1985), Nancy Reagan (1986), Dr. Denton Cooley (1987), and Michael Jordan (1990).

A Change in Leadership

In 1985 reaching the age of seventy, Father Hupp retired; he became executive director emeritus. In his thirteen years of leadership, Father Hupp's accomplishments were many: the introduction of family-style living for the boys; the addition of girls to the campus; construction of Boys Town's first youth care program outside Nebraska, and development of an inner-city alternative high school. To replace Father Hupp and carry on Boys Town's dynamic mission, the Board of Trustees called on Father Val J. Peter. After serving as deputy executive director for a year, he became Boys Town's fourth executive director in June 1985.

"Father Hupp was a great builder," said Father Peter. "He came at a time when child care in the United States was in disarray — terrible disarray. And his greatest achievement was putting into place a brand new childcare technology. He manned his pioneering effort with the best and the brightest people available. I only hope I do as good a job."

Father Val J. Peter, executive director of Boys Town since 1985.

A New Director

An Omaha native, Father Peter was educated at Holy Cross Grade School and Creighton Preparatory High School. It was while at Creighton Prep that he decided to become a priest. "One day, I forgot to bring my lunch," Father Peter recalled. "I was working in the school lunchroom and one of the Jesuits asked me: 'Aren't you going to eat your lunch?' I told him: 'I forgot it today, and I don't have any money.'

"The priest told me to follow him to the Jesuit dining room. I waited at the door. He came back outside and gave me a sandwich. I thought that was fabulous. So I ate the sandwich and I went to the chapel and I asked God to make me a priest like that."

After graduating from Prep, the aspiring priest spent two years at Immaculate Conception Seminary in Conception, Missouri. The next several years he studied in Rome at Gregorian University. He returned to Nebraska in 1966 with doctoral degrees in Theology and Canon Law. He taught at St. John Seminary in Elkhorn, Nebraska, College of St. Mary in Omaha, and finally at Omaha's Creighton University where he spent thirteen years on the faculty.

Charting the Past

After being named Boys Town's new director, Father Peter reflected on his predecessors: "Father Flanagan inspired people to give their lives to something far greater than themselves—namely the care of troubled children. A charismatic leader, he built Boys Town by the power of his personality and the attractiveness of his vision.

"After his death, no one could replace his charisma. So Boys Town needed someone with organizational skills to put all of that fire and vision into an orderly and disciplined move forward. Monsignor Wegner's achievement was to give organizational flesh and blood to Father Flanagan's dream. Right before he died, the troubles of America's children became radically different as the scourges of drugs, alcohol, suicide, sexual, emotional, and physical abuse infected many families. New methods, new treatments were required.

"Father Hupp's contribution to Boys Town, the development of a new model of youth care, was also uniquely important. There is nothing harder than vast organizational change."

From the beginning, Father Peter set his task as that of rekindling the fires of Father Flanagan's vision. He wanted Boys Town to rediscover the urgency and inspiration of Father Flanagan and his passion to help troubled children. "What was needed was someone to breathe fire back into the organization," Father Peter said as he embarked on a path of far-reaching change and expansion.

Setting New Goals

"When I arrived," explained Father Peter, "Boys Town was in residential care. We did it very well. But that's all we did. So I said to myself: 'We live in a fast-changing world. None of us knows what child care will look like twenty-five to fifty years from now. So we had better develop a continuum of care using these proven childcare technologies so that no matter what the troubles of children are in the future, something of the healing and hope Boys Town has pioneered will survive and be able to serve them.'"

Father Peter set a national goal for Boys Town of "changing the way America takes care of its children" before the year 2000. Achieving that goal required two radical changes: First, Boys Town would need to expand beyond a regional organization to a national organization. Second, there would need to be an expansion of Boys Town's childcare technology, moving beyond long-term residential care to the whole spectrum of child care including parent training, home-based services, shelter care, and treatment foster care.

Destination: America

The basic question about Boys Town's youth care program—was it replicable?—had begun to be answered at its first Boys Town USA site in Tallahassee, Florida. Encouraged by its success and the need and clamor for similar services for youth in many other cities, Father Peter planned a major and rapid expansion.

"We're taking our healing out from the heartland to the whole nation. It's a new manifest destiny," he said, announcing Boys Town's goal of establishing programs in seventeen major metropolitan areas by 1993. The first cities to join Tallahassee as Boys Town USA sites were Orlando, Florida; San Antonio, Texas; New Orleans, Louisiana; Las Vegas, Nevada; Brooklyn, New York; Portsmouth, Rhode Island; Delray Beach, Florida; Orange County, California; and Washington, D.C.

Since 1917 Boys Town had specialized in offering residential care to children who, for whatever reason, could no longer live with their families. Not all youngsters with family problems, however, needed to be removed and treated outside the home for long periods of time. Indeed it was often more beneficial to provide services to both parents and children while trying to keep the family together. In 1988 Father Peter took Boys Town's experience and transferred this technology to four new services—Parent Training, Home-Based Services (in-home crisis intervention), Treatment Foster Care, and Shelter Care. Under an umbrella called Family Based Programs, these services provided Boys Town's "continuum of care."

The long-term residential program and the four Family Based Programs operate at the Boys Town USA sites in a "hub-and-spokes" arrangement. Many sites have a mini-campus with three to five long-term residential homes as their "hub." One or more of the four "spoke" programs are also developed and put in place. Based on the service needs in each community, some Boys Town USA sites do not begin with residential homes but rather with one or several of the "spoke" programs only.

The Home Campus in the Village of Boys Town served as the pilot for the full

A New Orleans, Louisiana, youth care agency, Youth Alternatives, Inc., experienced financial difficulties in 1989 and asked Boys Town to take over its program. On October 1 Boys Town began operating three Youth Alternatives homes and its headquarters as a Boys Town USA site.

hub-and-spoke arrangement. Parent Training programs were first located at Offutt Air Force Base in Bellevue, Nebraska, Treatment Foster Care in Lincoln, Nebraska, Shelter Care in Grand Island, Nebraska, and Home-Based Services in Glenwood, Iowa.

A Continuum of Care

Abused, neglected, homeless, and runaway youth are given emergency care and counseling through the Boys Town Shelter Care Program. Throughout a child's stay in a shelter, Boys Town staff assess each family's situation and help the youth and family work toward reunification or alternative placement if needed. The first Boys Town shelter opened in temporary quarters in Grand Island, Nebraska, in March 1989. A permanent shelter was constructed and opened in 1991. Additional shelters were in operation in Sanford, Florida, and San Antonio, Texas, with others planned for Washington, D.C., and Long Beach, California.

Treatment Foster Care was launched in Lincoln in February 1986. It was expanded to Boys Town USA sites in Orange County, California; Orlando and Tallahassee, Florida; New Orleans, Louisiana; Brooklyn, New York, and Rhode Island. It features highly trained "treatment parents" who provide intensive twenty-four-hour care to youth who are unable to live at home or who have not been successful in traditional foster care programs.

The Home-Based Services program provides intensive in-home treatment to families in crisis. It seeks to keep families together and assist them in regaining control of their lives. Home-Based Services is designed to work with families with children who are at risk of placement outside their home. Trained family consultants provide families with eight weeks of in-home treatment and are on call around the clock for emergencies. In addition to the Glenwood location, a Home-Based Services program was also operating in Rhode Island, Southern California, and South Florida in 1992.

Offutt Air Force Base was the site of the first Parent Training program in February 1989. It teaches effective parenting skills to parents having difficulty with their children. The eight-week program uses lectures, discussions, role-playing, and frequent telephone contact to help parents build a healthy family environment. The service was also available in Delray Beach and Orlando, Florida, and San Antonio, Texas, in 1992.

This geographic and programmatic expansion meant that by 1992, its seventy-fifth anniversary year, Boys Town was taking care of more than sixteen thousand boys and girls in nine states and spending over eighty-four million dollars to do so.

Training Other Childcare Providers

The National Group Home Program, initiated in 1975, was expanded and renamed the National Training Center in 1989. Prior to this, technical assistance and training had been provided to other residential care facilities for youth so that they could fully replicate Boys Town's childcare technologies. Now, Father Peter wanted to influence more and more childcare providers, many of whom only wanted to use part of the Boys Town technology rather than all of it and others who worked with youth in schools and psychiatric hospitals rather than residential settings. Boys Town had developed a set of well-researched, outcome-oriented childcare technologies that actually changed the behavior of troubled children. It was time to start transferring these technologies to youth care providers working in other agencies and caring for children in different settings.

The National Training Center shares Boys Town's expertise in treating children who are emotionally or behaviorally disturbed, delinquent, or academically delayed through workshops, on-site training and consultation, and specialized materials. During 1991 the Center conducted workshops for childcare professionals from over three hundred organizations in ten major cities and trained educators from seventy-four school districts. In addition, the Boys Town Press was compiling Boys Town's youth care expertise into a series of publications and videotapes to help other childcare professionals, teachers, and parents themselves.

Research

The effectiveness of the Family Home Program and its components—training, consultation, evaluation, and administration—had been the result of ongoing research since 1973. It was this research that led directly to the healing of troubled children. To ensure the continuance of research and evaluation of all of Boys Town's expanded programs, in 1989 the Program Planning, Research, and Evaluation Department was organized to conduct research on the effectiveness of the residential, educational, and Family Based Programs. Also within the department is the Boys Town Reading Center that conducts research on literacy programs for the at-risk youth in Boys Town's middle and high schools, many of whom come to Boys Town with reading skills three to four years below their grade level. The goals of the department's researchers are first, to improve the care and education of Boys Town youth, and second, to disseminate knowledge about programs and innovations that prove to be effective to other professional and childcare audiences.

Boys Town National Hotline

In the late 1980s, despite Boys Town's impressive national expansion, there were still millions of troubled children and families who remained beyond the reach of Boys Town's direct care programs but who needed help just as desperately. So in May 1989 Father Peter established a lifeline to those troubled children and their parents—a toll-free crisis hotline number (1-800-448-3000) that was available to them twenty-four hours a day. Professional counselors for the Boys Town National Hotline handle calls on any problem, from drug abuse, sexual abuse, and suicide to depression and parent-child conflicts. After listening to the

The Boys Town National Hotline began taking crisis calls from children and parents in May 1989. An impressive list of celebrities such as Bill Cosby, Michael Landon, Hal Holbrook, Dick Van Dyke, Phil Collins, Jimmy Smits, and Nicolas Cage recorded radio and TV public service announcements for the Hotline.

caller's problems, the counselors offer initial advice and then, using a sophisticated computer database, refer the caller to agencies or services right in his or her own community for further help. In 1991 the Hotline received an average of over eleven hundred calls every day or more than four hundred thousand calls annually.

More Girls

Until 1985 the twenty-six girls residing at Boys Town had been a small presence amid a population of more than four hundred boys. Early in his tenure Father Peter decided to add as many girls as possible "to create a normal village with normal life." In 1986-87 ten new homes were built and eventually the four former dormitories were remodeled into twenty-two additional apartment homes for girls. By 1990 there were two hundred ten girls at Boys Town out of a total population of five hundred thirty-eight. Hundreds more girls were also being served by other Boys Town programs and in Boys Town USA site homes.

Such large numbers on the Home Campus produced systemic changes. The treatment model needed to be developed to take care of girls and their special needs and problems such as sexual abuse. Girls' athletic teams were formed. Girls had to be integrated into traditionally all-male activities such as the choir and band. Issues of appropriate friendship and dating skills had to be addressed.

These traumatic changes were not universally welcomed. Some thought them even "scandalous." Typical of the critics was one who predicted that "invariably when girls are turned loose so to speak they seem to 'go wild' to experience all their sexual desires." Father Peter pointed out that "girls get pregnant no matter where they live. Actually the girls who live here are much more protected and watched over. We have very, very strict rules, and (the boys and girls) abide by them." He reminded other critics that many girls who come to Boys Town have suffered sexual abuse. "Most of our kids are *victims* of crimes," he told them. "The girls tell us they feel safe here at Boys Town. Safe from the sexual exploitation and demands that they have experienced elsewhere. To this extent, they are free to be little girls again, free to grow up healthy and free to heal their past wounds."

Changes at Home

At the same time that Boys Town was expanding across the nation, other changes were taking place on the Home Campus. First, the former Grade School

In cooperation with the Nebraska Jewish Historical Society, Boys Town's Hall of History produced a traveling exhibit chronicling the friendship between Father Flanagan and Henry Monsky, longtime supporter and benefactor of the Home. Monsky's daughter, Joy Grossman, and two of his great-granddaughters attended the exhibit opening in February 1989.

Dining Hall was remodeled into a Hall of History to serve the hundred thousand visitors who annually come to tour the village. Plans to gather photographs, artifacts, and documents chronicling Boys Town's seventy years of history were put in motion early in the 1980s by Father Hupp. The Hall opened in 1986 in time to celebrate the one hundredth anniversary of the birth of Father Flanagan. Later that same year, Boys Town was designated a National Historic Landmark by the United States Department of the Interior. Also marking the date of Flanagan's birth was the issuance of a stamp in his honor by the U.S. Postal Service. The first-day-of-issue ceremony for the four-cent stamp in the "Great Americans" series was held on campus.

The Protestant Nativity Chapel in the Field House, built in 1953, had become too small and cramped for the expanding population of the Home which was approximately 60 percent Protestant. "Our Protestants," said Father Peter, "deserve just as nice a chapel as the Catholics."

The announcement that Boys Town would build a new Protestant chapel brought a spate of complaints: "You should be teaching children the Catholic faith." "I am deeply offended by your support of Protestantism." "The chapel will teach anti-Catholic ideas." Protestants are "hopping aboard a grand accomplishment of the Catholics." "I can't believe our donations are being used to build a Protestant chapel." As previous directors had done in the past, Father Peter reminded donors and the general public that Boys Town was nonsectarian and nonproselytizing; that it had always welcomed children of all faiths, encouraging and assisting them in the practice of their faith; and that the Protestant chapel would be funded by a single private donor, as the Catholic Dowd Chapel had been in the 1940s.

Funded by Raymond Chambers in memory of his father, the Herbert B. Chambers, Jr., Protestant Chapel for the Nativity of Our Lord is a cross-shaped Gothic structure. Completed in 1991, it seats four hundred people.

Vocational education at the Home dated back to the shoe repair classes taught to the boys in 1918. Seventy years later the complexity and computerization of the workplace had placed different demands on Boys Town's commitment to provide job skills to its students. A major renovation of the Vocational Career Center building and programs was mandated in 1988. Practical skills such as home maintenance and new courses in computer literacy and health sciences joined the curriculum in bright, updated surroundings. The excellence of Boys Town's educational program was recognized in 1989 when the high school was named one of "America's best" by President George Bush in a White House ceremony. The school was one of only two hundred eighteen nationwide to receive a U.S. Department of Education Secondary School Recognition Award.

The natural as well as the brick-and-mortar landscape of Boys Town was also changing. The Boys Town Environmental Education Plan was introduced in 1987. "Beauty is a silent teacher," said Father Peter. "Nature, God has set in our midst to teach us certain lessons we cannot learn elsewhere."

Boys Town youth actively participate in this plan through an agricultural education and training program. Different areas of the campus represent spring, summer, fall, and winter. The Garden of the Bible, located between the two chapels, is home for one hundred fifty species of plants mentioned in the scriptures, including olive and fig trees and the "burning bush." Horticulture training students help plant and care for thousands of square feet of flower beds and gardens on campus. Another aspect of the twenty-five-year plan is a wildlife habitat program, with nature trails and nesting boxes for wild birds. In addition, thousands of trees have been planted. In 1986 Boys Town was first designated a Tree City USA by the National Arbor Day Foundation, an honor it has received each succeeding year.

The Garden of the Bible in 1991 linked Dowd and Chambers Chapels on the campus. Pathways traced arches resembling chapel windows. Different areas of the garden featured plants from the Old and New Testaments.

To Help More Children

In 1972 Boys Town served seven hundred boys on campus. By 1992 more than sixteen thousand boys *and* girls were benefitting from direct care services at Boys Town sites around the country, including its hospital. In addition, there had been explosive growth in Boys Town's indirect services, in training and production of materials to help others help troubled children and families and in a hotline accessible to millions more. After Father Peter's first seven years as executive director, Boys Town had grown to become one of the greatest-ever private initiatives in child care. Its budget in 1985 was forty-one million dollars; by 1992 it was more than eighty-four million dollars.

"At Boys Town we feel there is a moral imperative urging us to help even more children," Father Peter explained. "Our children are on the edge of an abyss, a huge void created by economics and apathy. Unless we heal these boys and girls, we will soon be a nation not just of troubled children, but of lost children."

Driven by this "sense of urgency," Father Peter planned to continue Boys Town's expansion into new metropolitan areas through the 1990s. "Put simply," he said, "and borrowing from an unknown sage: 'If not us, who? If not now, when?'"

Past, Present, Future

Since Father Flanagan first opened his doors to homeless boys on December 12, 1917, more than eighteen thousand boys and girls have called Boys Town "home." In its first seventy-five years the dream of an Irish immigrant priest had grown to encompass a thirteen-hundred-acre village of homes, churches, and schools, programs and sites in nine states and the District of Columbia, nationwide training programs, a major research hospital, a model inner-city high school, and a national hotline available to millions more children and parents outside the reach of Boys Town's physical presence.

Could Father Flanagan have envisioned all that followed his first humble loan of ninety dollars rent money? Could he have foreseen the paths that each of his successors—Monsignor Wegner, Monsignor Hupp, and Father Peter—would take in leading Boys Town through succeeding decades? Perhaps not. For how could he have anticipated the rise in divorce rates, the plague of child abuse, the afflictions of surging drug use and alcoholism, the sexual revolution and frequency of teenage pregnancy, the crisis in education?

Whatever Father Flanagan mused about the future, however, he had been confident that Boys Town would endure. Shortly before his death, he was asked if there was anyone else dedicated enough to carry on his work with homeless and abandoned children. He replied, "The work will continue you see, whether I am there or not, because it is God's work, not mine."

The new eighteen-bed Midplains Shelter in Grand Island, Nebraska, was opened on July 13, 1991. At the close of 1991 Boys Town was operating other shelters in Sanford, Florida, and San Antonio, Texas.

A PHOTOGRAPHIC HISTORY

Marble-playing was one of the earliest forms of entertainment for the boys, playing here on the grounds of the German-American Home. It remained a popular sport at the Home into the 1940s when national tournaments were held on campus.

The boys dressed as pilgrims to march in the September 23, 1920, Ak-Sar-Ben Parade honoring the tricentenary of the *Mayflower* landing at Plymouth.

This photograph of Johnny Rushing, one of the Home's first residents, became a symbol of the "homeless boy," used by Father Flanagan in many of his early fund-raising appeals.

Father Flanagan bought Overlook Farm in May 1921 for a downpayment of a forty-acre farm in Florence, Nebraska, he had purchased earlier, plus seventy-five thousand dollars.

Food to feed two hundred hungry boys was sometimes scarce. One of Overlook Farm's previous owners had planted eighty-nine kinds of fruit trees and five types of grapes which continued to bear fruit and supplement the boys' diet.

In the spring of 1922 the boys began playing baseball almost daily. Readers of *Father Flanagan's Boys' Home Journal* were asked to contribute money for uniforms and transportation to other towns for games.

The one hundred sixty acres of farmland allowed Father Flanagan to harvest corn, alfalfa, clover, oats, potatoes, and vegetables, helping to feed the boys and the livestock.

Father Flanagan believed boxing was a good way for the boys to release energy and settle disputes, all within a set of rules.

Lack of equipment was a problem, but the boys managed to play football anyway.

In the early years the boys enjoyed an annual picnic and amusement rides at Krug Park, sponsored by various local women's organizations and businessmen.

From the very opening of the Home until the late 1960s various orders of nuns helped teach, nurse, cook, clean, and care for the boys. Here, they joined the boys for an outing at Krug Park.

One of the boys served some picnic fare to Father Flanagan seen in this photograph wearing his distinctive summer trademark, a strawboater.

The boys tried out their homemade sleds on an ice slide at Overlook.

Using scavenged instruments, Dan Desdunes, a well-known local bandleader, helped the boys learn to play and perform together. On December 23, 1921, the band played the opening and closing selections at the city's Christmas concert for four thousand people at the Auditorium.

Oscar Flakes was the band's drum major in 1925.

The boys went swimming in the sandpits at Valley, Nebraska, in June 1922.

Father Flanagan and some of the Home's volunteers and staff members in the early 1920s.

Hundreds of boys consumed many loaves of bread daily.

After a major fund-raising effort, Old Main was the first brick structure to be completed at Overlook.

Father Flanagan had very little money with which to hire staff in the early years, so the boys had to pitch in on many chores. Doing laundry was one of these tasks.

Father Flanagan instructing a class in Old Main.

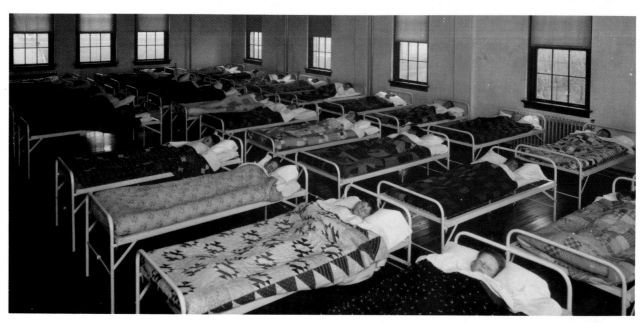

Old Main housed large dormitory rooms for sleeping. Colorful comforters and quilts were used on the beds on weekdays but were replaced by white blankets on Sundays.

Shoe repair was the first trade to be taught at the Home. The boys worked on this machinery in the late 1920s.

A typing class in 1929.

The band welcomed John Philip Sousa at Union Station in Omaha.

The young entertainers continued to travel the Midwest by train and by bus. On August 16, 1927, they played for President Calvin Coolidge at the Elks' Theater in Rapid City, South Dakota.

Johnny Rushing became known to thousands of radio listeners as "Johnny the Gloom Killer" as Father Flanagan turned to radio to spread the news about his boys' home.

In Omaha to play an exhibition baseball game on October 16, 1927, New York Yankee stars Lou Gehrig and Babe Ruth visited the Home, stayed for lunch, and then headed for the ballpark where the Home band played before and during the game. An orphan himself, Ruth visited Boys Town a number of times. During one trip, he autographed six baseballs for Father Flanagan to sell to raise funds for the Home.

In the 1930s the high school boys wrote and edited the Home's monthly publication, the *Journal*, and then printed it in their own print shop.

Boys played in the Old Main game room. What toys and games the boys had, they shared.

When boys became ill, they were cared for in the infirmary by the nuns and visiting physicians from Omaha. The Alexian Brothers later ran the Home's medical clinic from 1955 to 1976.

During the drought of 1933 the boys formed bucket brigades to water the vegetable gardens.

Meals were served communal-style in the basement dining room of Old Main.

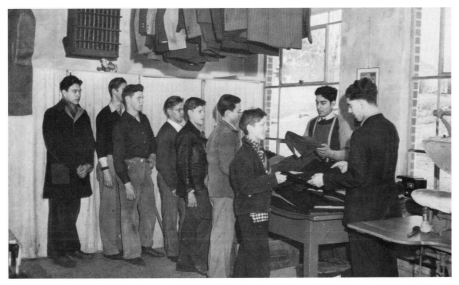

Student tailors Frank Caldron and Robert Mozingo helped supply the clothing needs of other boys on a busy Saturday afternoon in the campus tailor shop. The boys tailored their own graduation suits.

On December 27, 1934, the boys lined up to vote for a mayor and commissioners in Town elections in the library.

The boys celebrated Christmas with two days of fun and movies, no chores or school work. They all attended Midnight services and then opened gifts together in the play room. Some got packages from relatives; all received two presents each from Father Flanagan, often clothing, toothpaste or other toiletries, and fruit, nuts, and other treats from donors.

Boys of all faiths were welcomed to Boys Town. Each boy was required to study and practice his religion. Services were held in classrooms in Old Main.

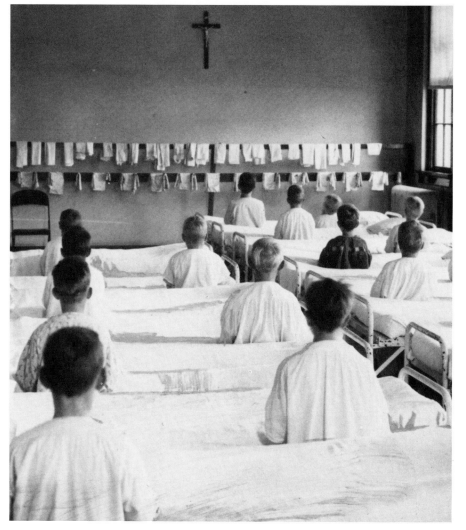

Patrick J. Norton, Father Flanagan's nephew and longtime staff member at Boys Town, was the village's first postmaster. At other times Norton served as business manager and historian for the Home.

Father Flanagan and one of his boys remembered the war dead on Decoration Day.

In August 1937 a fire of unknown origin destroyed a campus building that housed a horse stable, storage shed, and all of the boys' winter coats and clothing. Over the years, lightning caused a number of other fires in barns and wood frame buildings.

Mickey Rooney on campus in 1938 for the filming of "Boys Town."

Father Flanagan and Spencer Tracy chat during a break in filming. Tracy went on to portray the priest a second time in the sequel movie, "Men of Boys Town."

Many Boys Town residents served as film extras. Here, two of them entertained Rooney and Director Taurog.

Mickey Rooney signed autographs for young fans. The crowds of onlookers during the filming caused some problems, trampling the grass and flower beds and breaking tree limbs.

"Father Flanagan" and Boys Town citizens welcomed "Whitey Marsh" to the Home in a scene from the movie. Photograph courtesy Turner Entertainment Company.

Bobs Watson, who portrayed "PeeWee" in the movie, and Mickey Rooney reacted to the crowd at Union Station.

Thousands of people went down to Union Station to greet "Boys Town" stars arriving from Hollywood by train for the Omaha premiere of the film.

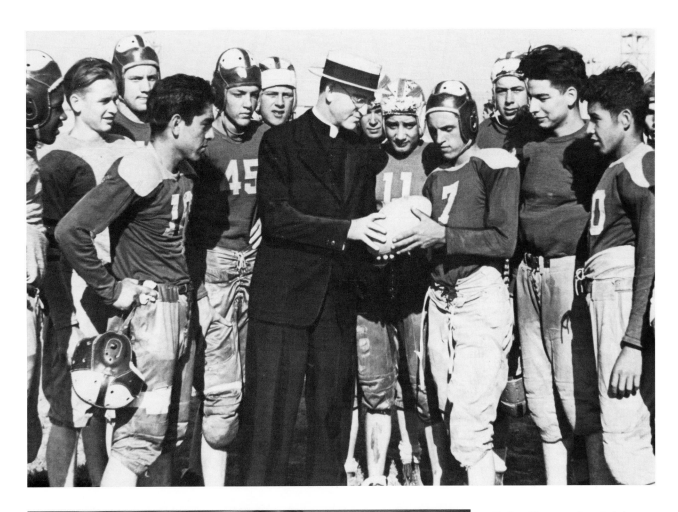

Father Flanagan handed the ball off to 1939 halfback Benny Jankowski. Spurred by the movie's publicity, Boys Town teams were soon playing before large crowds across the country.

Eagles Clubs nationwide raised money in a 1940 campaign to build new dormitories to house the growing numbers of boys. The Spokane, Washington, club displayed Boys Town honorary citizen certificates for all members who donated to the campaign.

In the foreground are the four new dormitories, including Eagle Hall, built in 1940. Behind them are the dining hall, the trade school and gymnasium, and Old Main. To the right of the dormitories, foundation work for Dowd Chapel had begun.

Moving day into the new dormitories. The building program allowed Father Flanagan to add one hundred twenty-four more boys bringing the Home's population to almost six hundred in 1941.

Father Flanagan and Henry Monsky, the commencement speaker, congratulate graduating seniors in 1942. Monsky was Flanagan's personal and the Home's attorney and a board member from 1929 until his death in 1947. He is the anonymous friend who loaned Father Flanagan the ninety dollars to rent his first home in 1917.

Father Flanagan visited the Army airfield in Sioux Falls, South Dakota, in May 1944. Seated with him in the jeep was Lee O'Hern, former Boys Town resident. During the war Flanagan was named America's No. 1 War Dad by the American War Dads organization because of the many Boys Town alumni serving in the Armed Forces.

Boys Town alumnus Joe Ortega and his Air Force "Spirit of Boys Town" plane. Ortega came home from the war, but forty-five other former boys were killed in action.

On the home front, Boy Scouts contributed to the war effort by collecting scrap metal on campus. The boys also planted a Victory Garden.

During a break in his travels Father Flanagan sang with the choir in Dowd Chapel.

In 1943 not all thoughts were of the war. These boys played Monopoly in one of the playrooms in the new dormitories.

Choir members, left to right, Clifford Fredericks, Robert Wright, Billy Williams, John Blake, Harold Kast, Wayne Sellars, Benny Markwell, and Anthony Tuzzio traced their fifty-city tour of America in 1946 with Choir Director Father Francis Schmitt.

The campus annually attracted thousands of visitors from around the world and provided a visitors' center where they could purchase a Boys Town souvenir, many of them made by the boys in their own ceramics shop.

Father Flanagan fished
with a young friend during
a trip to Miami in 1946.

A fire, starting in the attic, destroyed the roof of Old Main on January 3, 1947. The roof and later the facade were replaced, but the building was finally torn down in the 1970s.

Ten days before his death, Father Flanagan talked with a group of youngsters at the Austrian Youth Center in Vienna. U.S. Army Photograph

An aerial view of the Boys Town campus taken after the expansion building program planned by Father Flanagan and carried out by Monsignor Wegner.

Inside the new Dining Hall for high school students.

Twenty-five "cottages" were built to house the older boys. Choir members lived in this group of cottages named Caecilian Court.

Inside the cottages the boys were responsible for cleaning and other household tasks.

With the expansion of the physical plant, the Boys Town population grew larger through the 1950s, peaking at eight hundred eighty in the 1960s.

Jake Williams performed the high jump to an admiring crowd of onlookers at a track meet.

Members of the choir before a tour.

Monsignor Wegner helped distribute holiday gifts. Christmas celebrations had evolved into twelve days of festivities during Epiphany. The period was called "Twelfth Night" and featured movies, skits by both teachers and boys, caroling, and elaborate decorations.

Many Boys Town alumni went on to enlist in the military after high school graduation. Here, Geroyd Evans served as a fireman apprentice aboard the aircraft carrier U.S.S. *Valley Forge* in Korean waters in 1952. U.S. Navy Photograph.

Boys Town athletic teams enjoyed great success in the 1950s and 1960s. The football team was often ranked as one of the best in the nation. The 1956 basketball team celebrated a state championship with Coach Skip Palrang and Monsignor Wegner.

Monsignor Wegner with the children of St. Paul Orphanage in Seoul, South Korea, March 3, 1954.
As Father Flanagan had been, Wegner was often asked to travel and speak on child welfare issues. He also consulted with many foreign organizations wishing to found their own children's homes, modeled after the famous Boys Town.

Broadcasting the "Today" show from the campus on December 24, 1954. The show featured an appearance by the Boys Town Choir.

Actor James Garner as his TV character "Brett Maverick" visited the boys in September 1957.

The Junior-Senior Prom in 1962. Some of the boys invited their own dates to school dances. In addition, announcements of dances were posted at area high schools, and girls signed up to attend.

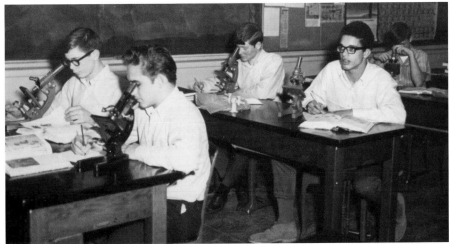

A biology class at the high school.

The Boys Town Field House was one of sixty Omaha centers for distribution of the Sabin Polio Vaccine in May 1962. Hundreds of boys, Boys Town employees, and many nearby city residents lined up for the vaccine.

The boys signed up for work details and part-time jobs at the Student Employment Office.

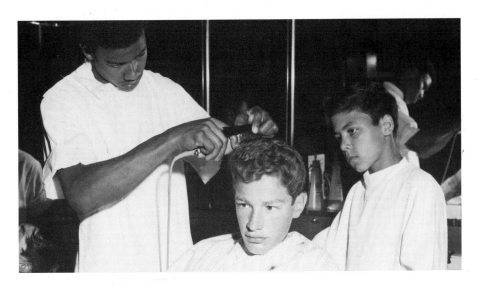

Mel Richardson, studying the barbering trade, cut the hair of sophomore Jerry Conrad.

Grade school students spent a quiet time reading.

Boys Town's Hi-Fives, made up of, from left, Jean Baladad, Carl Toon, Neil Olson, Scott Barnes, and Rick Durrett, played for the 1962 Homecoming Dance.

Boys Town citizens took an ice cream break while helping the surrounding neighborhoods of Millard and Westwood Park clean up after flood damage in June 1964.

A trio of varsity football players on the 1967 squad.

Vice President Hubert Humphrey delivered the commencement address and helped Monsignor Wegner hand out diplomas at graduation ceremonies in 1967.

On the Presidential campaign trail, Senator Robert F. Kennedy made a stop at Boys Town on May 13, 1968, just weeks before he was assassinated in Los Angeles.

In April 1969 former Boys Town resident, Commander Lloyd "Pete" Bucher of the U.S.S. *Pueblo*, accompanied by his wife, Rose, was welcomed home following his capture, imprisonment, and release by the North Koreans.

American prisoners of war in Southeast Asia were remembered by the boys in 1971 in a special Christmas display in one of the cottages.

At the 1971 Boys Town alumni reunion picnic, Monsignor Wegner talked with, from left, Wilburn Hollis, Bob Cross, George Burgess, and Bob Boucher.

Family-Teachers Ron and Annette Herron with the boys in their home at 116 Maher Circle.

The first recipient of the Father Flanagan Award for Service to Youth was Mrs. Spencer Tracy on June 25, 1975, for her work with hearing-impaired children. Omaha Archbishop Daniel Sheehan, left, helped Father Hupp present the award.

Father Hupp, appointed by President Gerald Ford to be a special U.S. representative to the United Nations during the International Year of the Child, listened to a U.N. debate in September 1976.

An octagonal shrine was added to Dowd Chapel in 1977 to house the tomb of Father Flanagan.

The Boys Town Choir posed on campus before one of their annual tours.

The Cadet Firefighters competed in the 1978 state tournament. The cadets regularly participated in regional and national competitions and came home often with trophies.

An enthusiastic outdoorsman, golfer, and hunter, Father Hupp's favored mode of transportation around Boys Town was the bicycle.

Basketball great Oscar Robertson was the featured speaker at the 1978 athletic awards banquet sponsored by the Boys Town Booster Club.

Patrick Norton and Mayor Barnaby Spring admired the new road sign honoring Norton for his many years of service to Boys Town. In 1979 the Village Board selected the names of alumni, longtime employees, Board of Trustees members, and supporters and assigned them to the previously un-named streets of the campus.

In May 1983 the first girls graduated from Boys Town High School.

For the first time in its history, Boys Town began fielding girls' athletic teams—junior varsity volleyball led the way. Cross country, basketball, and other sports followed.

A Boys Town trackman
visualized a victorious sprint.

A student tended the rose
garden, accredited by the All-
America Rose Selection
Committee and featuring
hundreds of donated bushes.
Throughout the 1980s the
horticulture program expanded
with more youths, more
gardens, and the addition of
the Vernon F. Dale Greenhouse.

Father Hupp and the choir presented a Two Brothers statue to Mayor Ed Koch on a 1983
visit to New York City.

The class of 1982
celebrated graduation.

Spiderman paid a visit to
BTNRH patients and staff.

Beginning in the early 1980s BTNRH offered a summer program for gifted hearing-impaired youth from around the country, designed to stimulate the learning potential and improve the self-esteem of these teenagers. Here, a group studied the formation of clouds.

Flanagan High students discussed the news with Principal Father James Gilg.

Boys Town's Father Flanagan High School opened in downtown Omaha in 1983 to serve inner-city youth at high risk of dropping out of regular high schools.

Flanagan High School students presented a Christmas program. Unlike many alternative schools, Flanagan offers a comprehensive program of extracurricular activities and athletic programs for its students.

Basketball player Julius Erving visited Flanagan High School in March 1984 after accepting the Father Flanagan Award for Service to Youth.

The first Boys Town home outside of the state of Nebraska opened in 1983 in Tallahassee, Florida, under Father Hupp's national Boys Town USA expansion program.

After many months of planning, construction of the new Hall of History got underway in 1985. Student employees and volunteers assisted by putting in hundreds of hours refurbishing artifacts, sorting photographs and documents, and helping build exhibits.

Larry Flanagan, nephew of Father Flanagan, provided the model for the face of the Flanagan figure on display in the Hall.

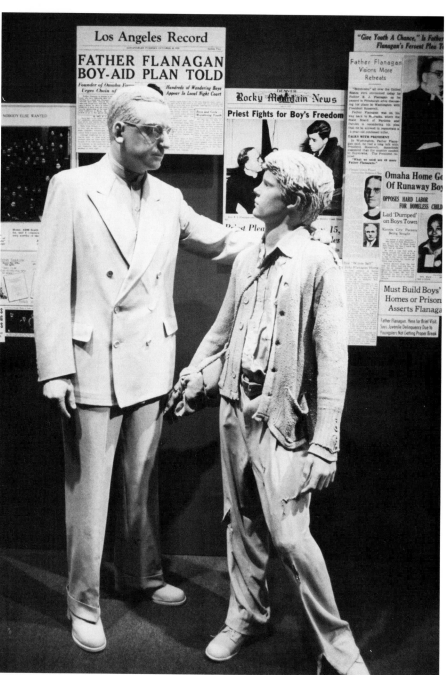

In November 1985 camera crews were back on the campus filming the television movie, "Miracle of the Heart: A Boys Town Story," starring Art Carney (right) and Casey Siemaszko.

Hundreds of Boys Town students including basketball players and cheerleaders, staff members, and their families helped fill a Field House gym to aid filming a scene for the TV movie.

Jane Pauley of NBC's "Today" show interviewed Father Val Peter in December 1985.

About thirteen hundred runners participated in Boys Town's first annual Memorial Day Run in 1985 on campus. The run is held each year to raise money for BTNRH's Center for Abused Handicapped Children.

The Voices of Boys Town, led by Music Director Frank Szynskie, sang the national anthem at Arrowhead Stadium in Kansas City to help kick off the November 9, 1986, game between the Kansas City Chiefs and the Seattle Seahawks.

First Lady Nancy Reagan was greeted on her visit to the campus on November 25, 1986, to accept the Father Flanagan Award for Service to Youth. During the presentation, her voice breaking with emotion and her eyes brimming with tears, Mrs. Reagan told the gathered boys and girls of Boys Town, "I know how good you are inside, and I would be proud to call you my own."

Boys Town youth visited with residents of the Val Haven Retirement Home in Valley, Nebraska, in 1986. Boys and girls must volunteer community service hours each year.

Physical education students worked out on new weight-training equipment at the Field House.

Every summer each Boys Town family spends two weeks at the Home's camp on Lake Okoboji in Iowa. The youth swim, fish, waterski, canoe, and enjoy other summer activities.

Alumni joined students for the 1987 campus reunion choir performance.

Old friends, Jake Williams, class of 1949, and Richard Watson, class of 1951, got together at the 1987 Alumni Convention.

In 1987 the Boys Town Band marched in the River City Roundup Parade in downtown Omaha behind a Home banner that dated back to at least 1940.

Gavin MacLeod, star of the "Mary Tyler Moore Show" and the "Loveboat," paid a visit to campus in November 1987.

Caroling outside a Family Home at Christmas. The Boys Town tradition of several weeks of special holiday events and celebrations continued into the 1990s.

Farm and 4-H activities were still popular in the 1980s. These youth celebrated completion of the fall harvest.

Other students learned and enjoyed the care and grooming of horses on the Boys Town Horse Farm. In a special program, Boys Town students taught horsemanship skills to a group of handicapped children.

Ryan White, a spokesman for young AIDS victims, talked to a high school class in March 1988.

Some of Boys Town's female residents helped celebrate the opening in April 1988 of five more newly constructed homes for girls bringing the total number of girls on the Nebraska campus to one hundred seventy.

In 1988 on the fiftieth anniversary of the "Boys Town" movie, "Whitey Marsh" (Mickey Rooney) and "PeeWee" (Bobs Watson) went another round on the Boys Town campus.

Boys Town youth volunteered their time and their hugs to help out at the annual Special Olympics held in the Field House.

Students worked in a computer classroom, part of the two million dollar remodeling of the Vocational Career Center, completed in October 1988. Computer literacy is just one of eight advanced areas of study a student may specialize in. Others are business services, health sciences, construction skills, electronics, barbering and cosmetology, food services, and automotive services.

In April 1989 the old student dormitory, Eagle Hall, re-opened as apartment homes for girls, and Boys Town coined a new version of Father Flanagan's well-known phrase.

Television personality Willard Scott gave his weather forecast for the "Today" show from Boys Town's Hall of History in March 1989.

Five new homes were under construction in March 1989 at the Boys Town USA site in San Antonio, Texas. The homes opened in June, and later Parent Training and a Shelter Care program were added to the Boys Town services available in San Antonio.

With ten newly constructed homes and remodeled apartment homes in several former dormitories, the number of girls on campus reached two hundred ten, providing plenty of candidates for cheerleading.

Stamps and coins donated to Boys Town had been on display in the PhilaMatic Center since the early 1950s. Exhibits were redesigned in July 1989 to appeal to children and the visiting public. Father Peter directed the stamp center, renamed for donor Leon Myers of Beverly Hills, California, to greatly expand its efforts to convert stamp donations to revenue to help support youth care programs.

President George Bush presents Mayor Robert Meraz with U.S. Department of Education Drug-Free School Recognition awards for Boys Town High School and Wegner School. At the White House ceremony on the south lawn, Bush called Boys Town "a healing balm that restores lost youngsters."

In December 1989 Boys Town opened its pilot Treatment Foster Care program in Lincoln, Nebraska, and began recruitment of foster parents.

A ceremony marked the laying of the cornerstone of the new Herbert B. Chambers, Jr., Protestant Chapel in October 1989.

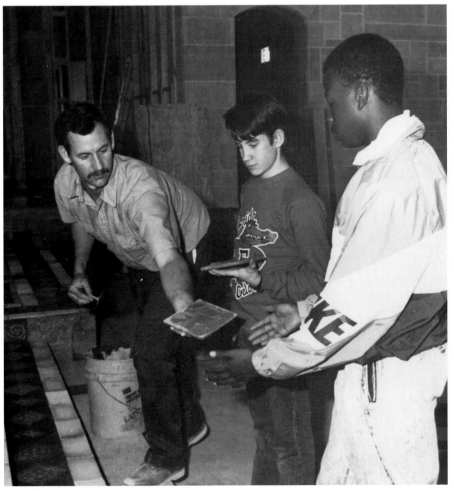

Students helped cement terra cotta tiles they and other Protestant youth at Boys Town had designed to the altar floor and steps in Chambers Chapel.

111

Twin angels added as the finishing touch to Chambers Chapel were dubbed "Hark" and "Herald."

Father Peter served up sandwiches at a picnic the evening before the May 22, 1990, dedication and opening of two more homes at Boys Town USA in Orlando, Florida. Orlando is a "super site" offering not only five long-term residential homes but a continuum of other services for families such as an emergency shelter, Parent Training, and Treatment Foster Care.

Professional basketball player Michael Jordan accepted the congratulations of a Boys Town student in the Music Hall where he received the Father Flanagan Award for Service to Youth on August 3, 1990. Jordan, the youngest ever to win the award, was honored for being a positive role model for youth, helping them stay in school and off drugs and alcohol.

Alumnus Ron Dennis, class of 1987, described his experiences in the Persian Gulf war to students at Wegner School in January 1991.

Father Peter was interviewed by local media at the April 1991 dedication of five new Boys Town USA-Nevada homes in Las Vegas. A shelter was also planned for the Las Vegas area.

A Christmas tree trimmed with yellow ribbons stood in Dowd Chapel during December 1990 to remind students of the thirty-three Boys Town alumni serving in the Middle East during the Persian Gulf war.

Sarah Williamson reacted to the announcement of her
precedent-setting election as Boys Town's first female mayor on May 5, 1991.

Students joined Father Peter for some Halloween fun at the Field House.

In 1991 three Boys Town USA sites were under construction. At left, five homes were planned for a seventy-six-acre site in Orange County, California. Treatment Foster Care and a Short-Term Residential Care facility in Long Beach were also underway. The aerial view at bottom left shows the twenty-acre site in Portsmouth, Rhode Island, donated to Boys Town USA. The New England program was scheduled to include long-term residential homes, Home-Based Services, and Treatment Foster Care. Site preparation had begun in 1991 on Boys Town USA-South Florida in Delray Beach (above). Programs to be offered included five homes for boys and girls and Parent Training.

During the 1991 Boys Town alumni convention, a new Armed Services Memorial on campus was dedicated to honor the more than two thousand former students who had served in all branches of the military.

A limited edition of two hundred fifty eggs designed by Theo Faberge was commissioned by Borsheim's Fine Jewelry and Gifts of Omaha. One of the amethyst crystal "Brotherhood Eggs" was donated to Boys Town on November 16, 1991, for display in its Hall of History. Mickey Rooney and Bobs Watson attended the special event.

An aerial view of the Boys Town campus, looking west, taken in 1990.

1917-1992
75
YEARS
BOYS & GIRLS
FATHER FLANAGAN'S
BOYS TOWN
1917-1992
75
YEARS

The Voices of Boys Town performed at the dinner hosted by Borsheim's to present the Brotherhood egg and to kick off Boys Town's seventy-fifth anniversary year.

February 3, 1918
First issue of *Father Flanagan's Boys' Home Journal* is printed.
Edward Ditz wins a new suit of clothes as the boy selling the most copies.

A BOYS TOWN TIMELINE

1910s

December 12, 1917
With a borrowed ninety dollars, Father Flanagan rents a home at Twenty-fifth and
Dodge streets in downtown Omaha and officially opens Father Flanagan's Boys' Home.

June 1, 1918
Father Flanagan's Boys' Home moves to the abandoned
German-American home on Thirteenth Street.

July 13, 1918

Boys help Father Flanagan celebrate his birthday with a festival of music and dramatic skits.

August 1918

The Home's first trade classes begin when "Mr. Joe" helps open a shoe repair shop in the basement of the Home.

October 1918

A deadly Spanish influenza epidemic rages through Omaha. Twenty boys fall ill.

November 1918

Women in St. Patrick's Parish organize a sewing club to make and mend clothes for the boys.

April 27, 1919

The Home's baseball team wins its season opener with St. Rose Parish, 6-5.

June 17, 1919

The boys attend their first annual picnic at Krug Park. Games include a fifty-yard dash and pie-eating contest.

1920s

August 1920

Knights of Columbus sponsor a tour of Nebraska by Father Flanagan and an entertainment troupe of five boys.

December 23, 1920
The Christmas program includes skits, chicken, and ice cream for dinner, stockings, packages, and a tree decorated and donated by the Mothers' Guild.

March 29, 1921
Father Flanagan sends his first letter appealing for funds to support the Home to Catholic residents in eastern Nebraska and western Iowa.

May 18, 1921
Overlook Farm, ten miles west of Omaha, is purchased as the future site of the Home.

August 16, 1921
Juvenile Entertainers troupe performs for inmates at Leavenworth, Kansas, Penitentiary.

September 15, 1921
Father Flanagan's Boys' Home Band, conducted by Dan Desdunes, gives first concert at St. Rose's Church.

September 20, 1921
Boys march in Omaha's Ak-Sar-Ben Floral Parade.

March 30, 1922
Ground is broken for a new five-story main building.

September 1925
Two local businesses donate a new gateway arch for the Home's entrance.

October 22, 1921

The Home completes the move to Overlook Farm.

November 14, 1921

Father Flanagan begins three hundred thousand dollar fund drive for permanent buildings.

December 1921

By the end of the year, one hundred twenty-five boys are living at the Home.

May 1922

Boys churn over two hundred pounds of butter and nearly two hundred pounds of cottage cheese during May on the dairy farm.

November 10, 1922

Boys celebrate "Pie Day" at the Home by eating thirty-seven ten-inch pies.

January 26, 1923

Traveling for the first time in its own Pullman railroad car called "Overlook," the band leaves on a one-month tour of Iowa and Missouri.

February 1, 1923

The Home's broom factory opens and in special "broom races," Mike Jankis is the best at straw sorting while Fred Barnes wins the dyeing contest.

January 1924

Typewriters have arrived, and typing classes are scheduled to begin soon.

January 1926

Father Flanagan and the band begin weekly radio shows, "Advice to Boys," on Mondays at 6 p.m. on WAOW. In April, the show moves to Sunday afternoons and is called "Father Flanagan's Boys' Period."

February 14, 1926

Boys vote to officially change the name of Overlook Farm to "Boys Town." William Roach is elected first student mayor.

October 16, 1927

New York Yankees Babe Ruth and Lou Gehrig tour the campus, beginning the long parade of celebrities, sports stars, and political figures to visit the Home through the years.

May 1928

Two hundred boys enter the *Omaha Bee News* marble contest. Francis Studer is the Home's champion and advances to the city contest.

August 3, 1928

The Juvenile Entertainers' troupe performs for President Coolidge at his summer quarters in Superior, Wisconsin.

January 1928

Fans of radio's "Johnny the Gloom Killer" form the National Gloom Killers Club. Will Rogers is elected first club president.

April 10, 1928

Cowboy actor Tom Mix visits Boys Town.

1930s

March 1, 1930

William McGinn, a Boys Town eighth grader, wins the Douglas County spelling bee.

March 2, 1930

Fire destroys the power and laundry buildings, barn, and corn crib.

May 5, 1932

Boys Town holds its first track meet with various trade school classes competing against each other.

August 1932

Father Flanagan's Boys Home Journal reports the Home is perilously near closing in the midst of the Depression. The public is asked to help.

November 1932

Presidential candidate Franklin Roosevelt and his wife, Eleanor, tour Boys Town, declaring it to be "one of the most beautiful places" visited on their trip.

August 1934
Jimmie Webster, Boys Town resident, creates the Homeless Boy statue which is put on display.

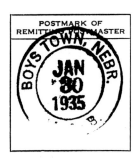

December 6, 1934
Boys Town Post Office opens with Patrick J. Norton as postmaster.

November 27, 1932
As usual on the last Sunday of the month, the Home holds a party—this time, for all boys with November birthdays.

July 4, 1933
The holiday starts forty-five minutes later than normal as the boys are allowed to "sleep in." Activities include a baseball game, swimming and races, an outdoor picnic of chicken, root beer, and ice cream, followed by a Charlie Chaplin movie in the auditorium.

August 1933
Boys form water brigades to save the vegetable gardens, but drought destroys the oat crop, nineteen acres of potatoes, and a hundred acres of corn.

September 1934
Another year of drought destroys three hundred twenty acres of crops and gardens.

January 15, 1935
Boys elect Tony Villone as mayor of Boys Town.

August 4, 1936
Boys Town becomes an incorporated village by vote of the Douglas County commissioners.

September 1936
For the first time, Boys Town opens the school year with a complete four-year high school course. Classes offered include English, algebra, Latin, general science, geometry, physics, economics, American and world history.

October 18, 1936
The Boys Town Choir makes its debut in a concert held at the Joslyn Memorial in downtown Omaha.

November 20, 1936
Boys Town Mayor Daniel Kampan meets in New York City with Mayor Fiorello LaGuardia.

December 1937
The Welfare Department reports that boys from twenty-eight states were residents at the Home in 1937.

March 1938
J. Walter Ruben and Dore Schary of MGM visit Boys Town to review movie script with Father Flanagan and throw an ice cream party for the boys.

November 1936

Boys choose delegates to visit Father Flanagan at home during his illness and report on his progress.

September 7, 1938

"Boys Town" premieres at the Omaha Theatre. Crowds fill downtown streets to catch a glimpse of stars Spencer Tracy and Mickey Rooney.

November 26, 1938

The Boys Town Blues football team defeats Black Foxe Military Academy (school of many Hollywood film star children), 20-12, in California.

December 1938

The Home's population is now close to two hundred boys.

June 26, 1938

Cast and crew of "Boys Town" begin filming.

February 23, 1939

Spencer Tracy wins the Academy Award for his performance in "Boys Town." He later gives his Oscar to Father Flanagan.

April 1940

Boys consume ninety pounds of milk and one hundred loaves of bread daily.

June 14, 1940

After entertaining the boys with a thirty-minute show, Gracie Allen is named honorary mayor, and George Burns, an honorary citizen.

June 28, 1940

Boys move into new dormitory apartments and eat in the new dining hall.

November 1940

MGM begins production of "Men of Boys Town," a sequel to the hugely successful 1938 movie.

December 1941

Father Flanagan creates the Foundation Fund, an investment fund he hopes will one day make the Home self-sufficient and no longer dependent on annual appeals to donors.

January 5, 1941

Dowd Memorial Chapel of the Immaculate Conception, donated by Marie Dowd of New York City, is dedicated.

December 7, 1941

Former Boys Town residents, George Allen Thompson, William Debbs, and Donald Monroe, die in the attack on Pearl Harbor—the first of more than forty-five former boys to lose their lives fighting in World War II.

December 21, 1941

CBS Radio airs the first of several national broadcasts of the Boys Town choir.

July 1942

Bud Abbott and Lou Costello perform for the the boys. They visit Boys Town again in 1943 and donate baseball uniforms to the Home.

December 10, 1942

The Home celebrates its first twenty-five years. President Roosevelt sends congratulations.

January 16, 1944

High school graduation is held early as part of the wartime accelerated program.

August 1944

More than one hundred boys spend the summer working in the Boys Town Victory Garden.

October 22, 1944

A crowd of 43,539 attends the Boys Town-Detroit Central Catholic football game, the largest game attendance in the country that day, according to the *Detroit Times*. Game ends in a 14-14 tie.

January 25, 1946

Boys Town announces a thirty million dollar expansion that will double the size of the Home, adding an administration building, high school, twenty-five cottages, visitors center, dining hall, field house, music hall, and vocational career center.

February 8, 1946

Alumnus Robert Paradise visits campus and tells of his forty-one months as a prisoner of war, captured by the Japanese during the fall of Bataan.

June 14, 1946

The campus Boy Scouts start a drum and bugle corps.

July 12, 1946

A course in automotive mechanics is added to the trade school curriculum.

October 25, 1946

Under the direction of Father Francis Schmitt, the Boys Town Choir opens its eight-week tour with a concert for nine thousand people in St. Paul, Minnesota. New York's Carnegie Hall is a future stop.

April 7, 1947

At the invitation of the War Department, Father Flanagan tours Asia, investigating the need for aid to war orphans and meeting with Gen. Douglas MacArthur.

May 15, 1948

On a child welfare mission to Germany, Father Flanagan dies in Berlin.

May 21, 1948

Following two funeral Masses on campus, Father Flanagan's body is entombed at Boys Town.

June 5, 1948

President Truman visits Boys Town and lays a wreath at the tomb of Father Flanagan.

September 1948

The older boys move into twenty-five new cottages, part of the thirty million dollar expansion program.

September 15, 1948

Msgr. Nicholas H. Wegner is named executive director of Boys Town to succeed Father Flanagan.

September 10, 1949

The first Boys Town Royal Livestock Show is held in the Field House.

December 1949

Football coach Maurice "Skip" Palrang is named national Pop Warner Coach of the Year, following a 9-1 season.

July 11, 1947
Father Flanagan reports findings of his Asian trip to President Harry Truman at the White House.

November 28, 1948
A statue of Father Flanagan and four boys, given by Variety Clubs International, is dedicated on campus.

1950s

January 1950

With the building expansion complete, seven hundred eighty-eight boys are now in residence at the Home.

July 1, 1951
The Boys Town PhilaMatic Center, housing a donated collection of stamps, coins, and paper money, opens.

December 24, 1951
CBS television broadcasts Midnight Mass from Dowd Chapel nationwide.

January 23, 1954
The *Saturday Evening Post* tells the story of "The Boy Who Walked to America," Joseph Anthony. A Korean war orphan with artificial feet, Anthony was befriended by American GIs who wrote to Msgr. Wegner on his behalf. Anthony arrived at Boys Town in June 1953.

February 1954
Msgr. Wegner leaves on a five-month governmental goodwill tour of Asia.

June 1954
The Boys Town Cowboys capture their first Nebraska Class A state track championship.

August 13, 1954
"Voice of America" reporters spend a day at Boys Town recording interviews to air behind the Iron Curtain.

November 1954
World heavyweight boxing champion Rocky Marciano visits the boys.

February 1955
Boys Town purchases a new fire truck for the volunteer fire department formed in 1946.

February 10, 1950
The boys travel to Lincoln as guests of Gene Autry to attend his show at the coliseum and to eat dinner in the Cornhusker Hotel ballroom.

December 1951
The Boys Town National Alumni Association is organized.

June 18, 1952
Duncan Reynaldo, otherwise known as TV's "Cisco Kid," visits the campus.

November 1956

Former Boys Town resident, Charles "Deacon" Jones, finishes ninth in the Olympic steeple-chase held in Melbourne, Australia.

April 1966

The Cowboy cagers win their second state basketball championship in a row.

March 1958

Msgr. Wegner appears on the television show, "To Tell the Truth," but he can't stump the celebrity panel of Polly Bergen, John Cameron Swayze, Kitty Carlisle, and Hy Gardiner.

1960s

June 1962

Indira Gandhi, daughter of India's Prime Minister Nehru, visits the Home.

October 1962

The choir records an album of Christmas music with the Everly Brothers.

August 1964

Nearly two hundred of the boys help nearby residents clean up after severe flood damage in western Omaha.

December 1964

Richard Coyle wins the campus cribbage tournament.

September 1965

Boys Town High School joins the newly organized Metropolitan Athletic League of Omaha and Council Bluffs, Iowa, schools.

December 1965

The first issue of *The Lariat* a campus student newspaper, comes off the press.

May 28, 1967

Vice President Hubert Humphrey delivers the fiftieth anniversary commencement address.

December 10, 1967

A bust of Father Flanagan is unveiled in the Nebraska State Hall of Fame.

January 23, 1968

The U.S.S. *Pueblo*, commanded by former Boys Town resident Lloyd Bucher, is taken captive by the North Koreans. After his release, a big welcome home ceremony is held at Boys Town on April 24, 1969.

1 9 7 0 s

September 1970

As part of a pilot program permitting limited off-campus employment for Boys Town citizens, twenty-two boys are hired by Walgreen Drug Stores.

June 1971

Bryan Ladner, Boys Town junior, is Omaha's Student Volunteer of the Year for giving more than five hundred work hours to St. Vincent Retirement Home.

March 30, 1972

The *Omaha Sun* newspapers report Boys Town's net worth to be over two hundred million dollars. The Board of Trustees launches a yearlong study with the help of outside consultants that results in expansion of Boys Town programs.

April 1972

After twenty-nine years as head football coach with a record of 201 wins, 66 losses, and 12 ties, Athletic Director Skip Palrang retires.

September 15, 1973

Msgr. Wegner retires as Boys Town Executive Director.

May 6, 1975

Boys Town residents help Omaha clean up after a devastating tornado hits the city.

February 1976

In tribute to the country's bicentennial, the Boys Town Choir produces a record, "Boys Town Sings America."

March 18, 1976

Former Boys Town executive director Msgr. Nicholas H. Wegner dies in Omaha.

October 11, 1973
Father Robert P. Hupp is named to replace Msgr. Wegner as executive director.

May 1976
Campus cottages are remodeled into "Family Homes" to house the boys. Construction begins on sixteen new homes. The family-style program is phased in to replace dormitory living.

May 4, 1976

Mother Teresa of Calcutta is awarded the Father Flanagan Award for Service to Youth.

May 1, 1977

The Father Flanagan Shrine, newly built resting place of Father Flanagan's tomb, is dedicated.

July 31, 1977

Boys Town Middle School is renamed to honor former director Nicholas Wegner.

September 9, 1977

The Boys Town Institute, later renamed the Boys Town National Research Hospital, opens to provide treatment to boys and girls with hearing and speech disorders. It is the first time girls are treated by a Boys Town program.

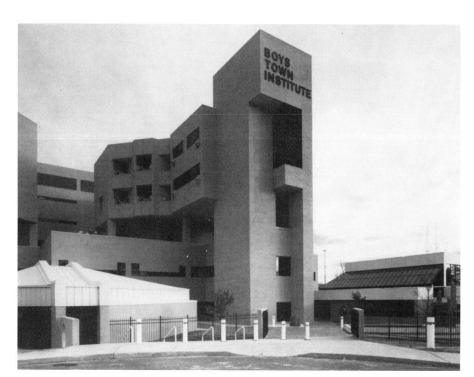

April 6, 1979

The first girl is admitted as a resident of Boys Town.

August 6, 1978

Nebraska places a state historical marker honoring Boys Town on the campus.

May 6, 1979

The Boys Town Choir performs on the Osmond Family television show.

1980s

May 29, 1983

The first five girls graduate from Boys Town High School. There are fifteen girls in residence on campus.

August 1983

First Boys Town USA site opens with one home in Tallahassee, Florida.

September 1983

Father Flanagan High School in downtown Omaha is opened. Formal dedication takes place on October 23.

April 1984

Wegner School students perform in a variety show for their classmates.

July 1985

Boys Town is named a National Historic Landmark by the U.S. Department of the Interior.

November 1985

Filming of the TV movie, "Miracle of the Heart: A Boys Town Story," starring Art Carney is underway on campus.

August 2, 1986

Boys Town Fire Cadets win first place in the National Fire Cadet Competition.

September 1986

Barbara Bush, wife of the Vice President, visits with Wegner School students as part of her campaign to combat illiteracy.

November 25, 1986

First Lady Nancy Reagan comes to Boys Town to accept the Father Flanagan Award for Service to Youth.

June 15, 1985

Father Hupp retires as executive director and Father Val J. Peter is appointed to lead Boys Town.

March 14, 1986

The Boys Town Hall of History, chronicling the Home's story with photographs, artifacts, and videos, opens.

April 8, 1988

Five more new homes for girls open. There are now one hundred seventy girls living on the Home campus.

July 11, 1988

Mickey Rooney and Bobs Watson return to campus to help celebrate the fiftieth anniversary of the movie, "Boys Town."

March 1989

Boys Town's Family Based Programs opens its first shelter in a rented building in Grand Island, Nebraska. Plans are underway to build a new shelter close to Interstate 80.

July 14, 1986

The U.S. Postal Service holds the first day of issue ceremony for its new four-cent Father Flanagan stamp at Boys Town, one hundred years after Flanagan's birth in Ireland.

October 23, 1986

The second Boys Town USA site in Florida opens with three homes in Orlando.

April 3, 1987

Five new homes for girls, part of an on-campus ten-home expansion, are completed, adding forty more girls in residence, bringing the total to one hundred thirty.

April 7, 1989

Former dormitories are remodeled and open as new homes for girls. There are now more than two hundred girls in residence on campus.

June 1989

A Boys Town USA site of five homes opens in San Antonio, Texas.

July 29, 1989

The Leon Myers Stamp Center opens with new exhibits on the history of postage, the Father Flanagan stamp, and children's issues.

October 1, 1989

Boys Town USA dedicates three homes for children in New Orleans, Louisiana.

December 6, 1989

Boys Town's pilot Treatment Foster Care program gets underway in Lincoln, Nebraska.

May 3, 1989

Glenwood, Iowa, is the location of the first Home-Based Services Program, in-home counseling and treatment for families in crisis.

October 22, 1989

The Boys Town National Hotline begins toll-free crisis telephone service to all fifty states and the District of Columbia. Dozens of TV actors, film stars, and sports celebrities agree to record public service announcements to help publicize the hotline.

December 12, 1989

Father Peter announces plans for a Boys Town USA site in Orange County, California.

---

1 9 9 0 s

April 3, 1990

Boys Town opens its second shelter in Sanford, Florida, to serve children in central Florida.

May 22, 1990

The fourth and fifth homes built on the Boys Town USA site in Orlando, Florida, are opened and dedicated.

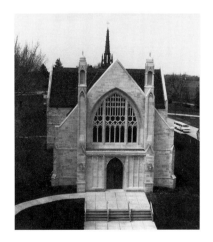

June 24, 1990

The new Protestant Gothic-style chapel, donated in memory of Herbert B. Chambers, Jr., of New Jersey, is dedicated.

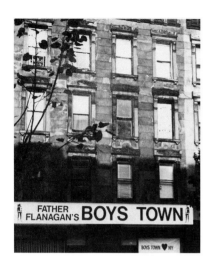

October 11, 1990
Boys Town's New York site opens in a renovated Brooklyn brownstone. Six girls are in residence. Two more homes are planned.

November 16, 1991
Mickey Rooney visits Boys Town to help Borsheim's Fine Jewelry and Gifts unveil a limited edition egg, designed by Theo Faberge, featuring the famous "Two Brothers" symbol.

August 3, 1990
In a campus ceremony, basketball player Michael Jordan accepts the Father Flanagan Award for Service to Youth.

September 10, 1990
Vice President Dan Quayle visits the campus.

October 12, 1990
Boys Town announces it will build a Boys Town USA site to serve New England on a donated twenty-acre piece of property in Portsmouth, Rhode Island.

April 26, 1991
Five new homes for boys and girls are dedicated at the Boys Town USA site in Las Vegas, Nevada. This brings the total of residential homes in operation to one hundred in six states, with a thousand children in Boys Town's direct care programs operating in nine states.

May 5, 1991
Sarah Williamson is elected mayor, the first girl to hold the post in Boys Town history.

May 6, 1991
Part of ABC-TV's "Good Morning America" program is broadcast from the Boys Town campus. The new mayor is interviewed.

July 27, 1991
Four hundred alumni gather on campus for a reunion and to dedicate a new Alumni Armed Services Memorial.

December 12, 1991
Boys Town begins celebrating its seventy-fifth anniversary year.

January 23, 1992
At a news conference in Washington, D.C., Father Peter announces that Boys Town will open an emergency short-term residential center for troubled boys and girls in the District of Columbia.

Dates in the timeline have been reconstructed as accurately as possible from issues of *Father Flanagan's Boys' Home Journal, Boys Town Times, Boys Town Quarterly,* and other publications, correspondence, and documents in the Boys Town Hall of History.

INDEX